Faith Unlimited

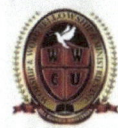

Faith Unlimited e-magazine is published
By World International Bible Training Center
AKA
Bill Hanshew Ministries,
a non-profit corporation.

PO Box 397
Rolla, MO 65402

Volume 5
Issue 6
June 2018

Faith Unlimited is a free online Magazine and has no Subscription price and is Supported through contributions from readers worldwide.
Gifts to this ministry are tax deductible as allowed by the IRS

All Rights Reserved

All rights regarding this e-magazine, Faith Unlimited, are reserved. Reproduction of any part of this magazine without the written permission of Faith Unlimited Staff is prohibited.

While the views expressed in Faith Unlimited do not necessarily reflect the policy of the government, no official endorsement should be inferred. All views and comments expressed in Faith Unlimited are solely the opinions of the writers and not necessarily the opinions of the readers.

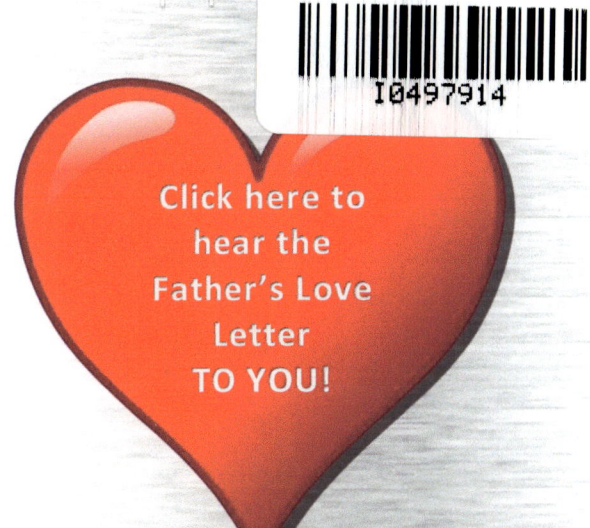

Click here to hear the Father's Love Letter TO YOU!

Wow! Did you listen to the Letter from the Father to you? If not, and it won't allow you to click on the heart, here is the link: https://youtu.be/qpSE3eZTCNo ... Please listen to it.

I'm sure some of you Fathers may not have had the love of a Natural Father that you deserved to have, but Father God loves you unconditionally. This is the main message we need to get to hurting people. Even sometimes children hide their feelings from their parents. Why? Maybe they are afraid of the outcome if they tell them things that someone told them not to tell. Fathers, show your children God's love. Let them know that it is ok to come to you with any kind of problem, and that you will be there for them, just like our Heavenly Father is to you.

I do hope you will take the time to look through this month's issue of Faith Unlimited. I am very proud of Lance Smith, my featured writer this month. He was a young person in a church where we were youth leaders at the time. He has grown into a wonderful young man who loves God with all his heart, and he shares his story in this issue. It is called, "*Talent is Cheap, but Dedication is Costly.*" God has truly blessed him with many talents!

Also, in this month's issue we celebrate Grace International Bible University's 1st year Anniversary! I work with GIBU, based out of Liberia, Africa, and I can personally say it is growing leaps and bounds day by day. The 5 Continents are hearing about the "FREE TUITION" and are taking advantage of this great offer! But the important thing that I can share is that everyone I have had contact with, whether staff, professor, or student, they have a heart for God. They are from all over the world and love each other!

Please take the time to look through the pages and pray for those who write articles, those who have ads, and for GIBU. And if this magazine blesses you, please text me – faye.faithunlimited@gmail.com or drop me a note on Facebook!

God Bless all of you, and Happy Father's Day to all of you Dads!

Faye Hanshew

Publisher and Editor

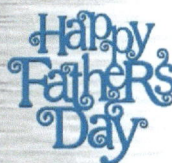

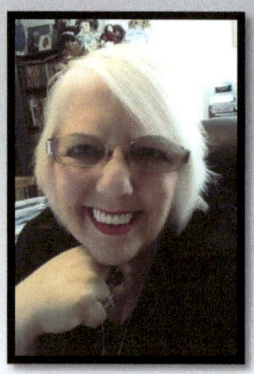
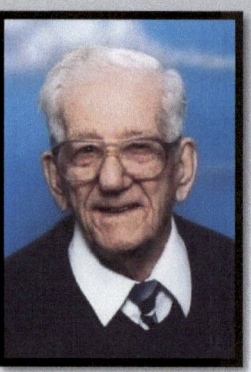
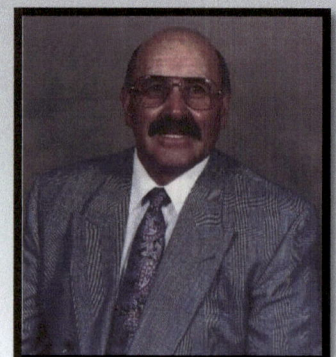
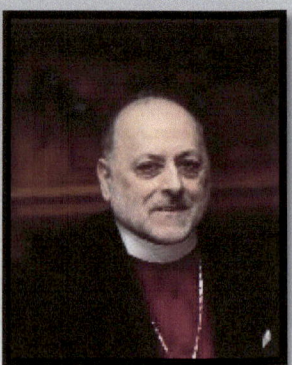

Publisher & Editor
Faye Hanshew

Faye's Father

Bill's Father

Co-Publisher & Co-editor
Dr. Bill Hanshew

Meet Lance	Annette Smith
Talent is Cheap, but Dedication is Costly	Lance Smith
I Died When He Died	Dr. Bill Hanshew
Grace International Bible College – 1st Anniversary Section	Faye Hanshew and Dr. Rudolph Q. Kwanue
God's Lawnmower	Genice Fulton
No More Texting the Dead Man – Part 2	Matthew Deves
Do We Fear Death – Of the Old Man?	Dr. Richard Rundell
Understanding Salvational Vocabulary – Part 2	Dr. John Roberts
Just Words?	Dewanshu Ahlawat
The Father-Heart of God	Pastor Jo Bruns
Favor for Favor	Author/Speaker Larry Thompson
Die No More	Evangelist Ernest Kweku Nanor
The Deeper Life	Steve Porter

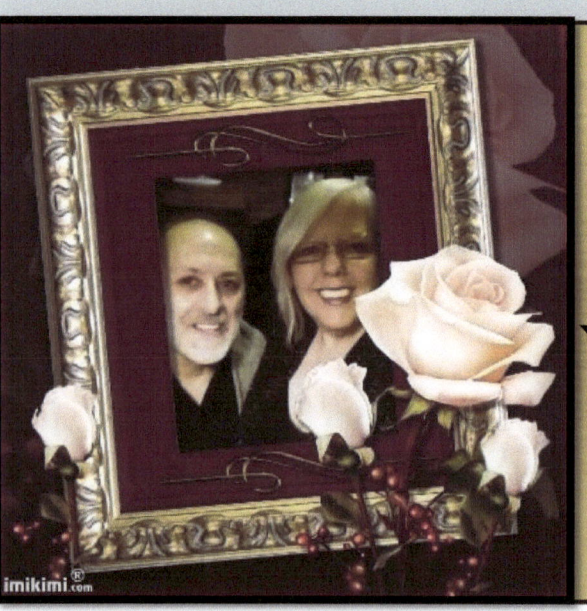

Happy
Father's Day
Father of My Children
You are the source of my joy,
The Center of my World!
I love You!
Faye

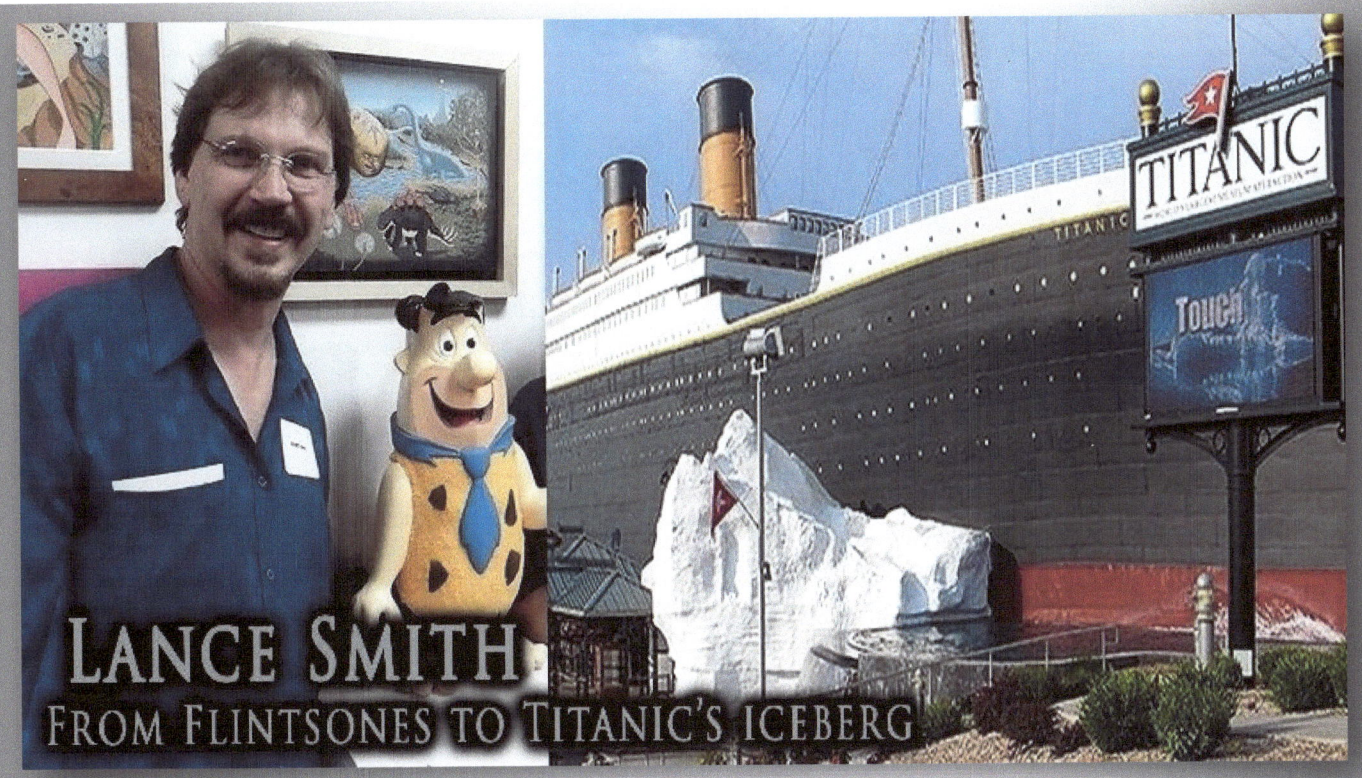

SCULPTURER

SINGER

SERVANT

SONGWRITER

ARTIST

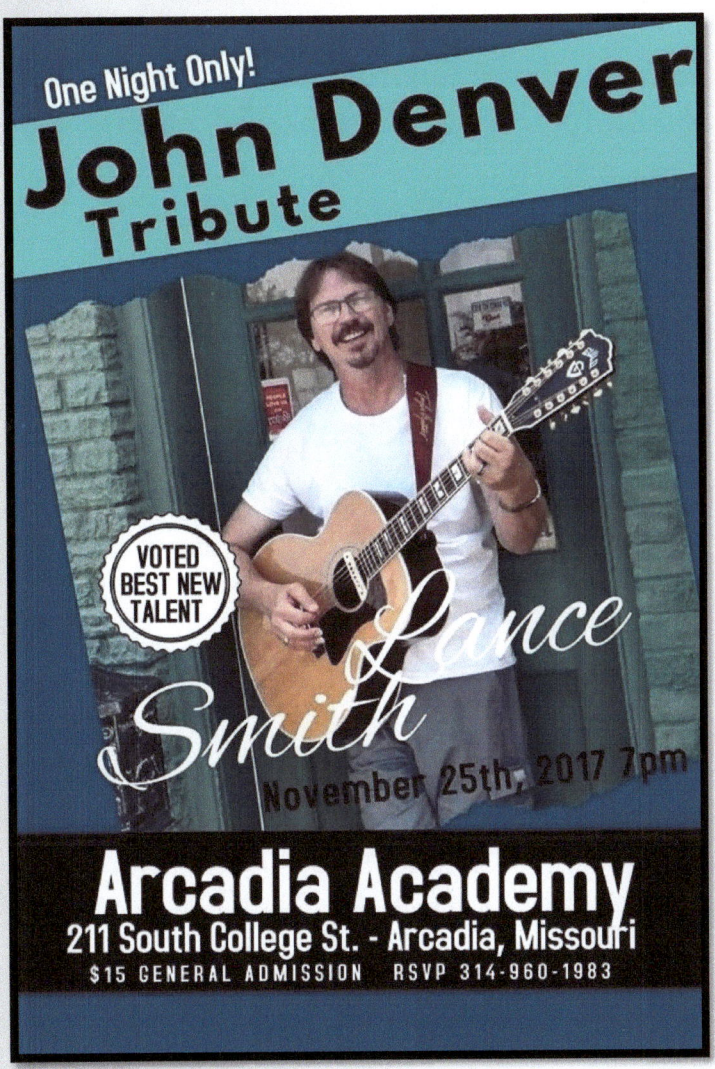

MEET LANCE SMITH

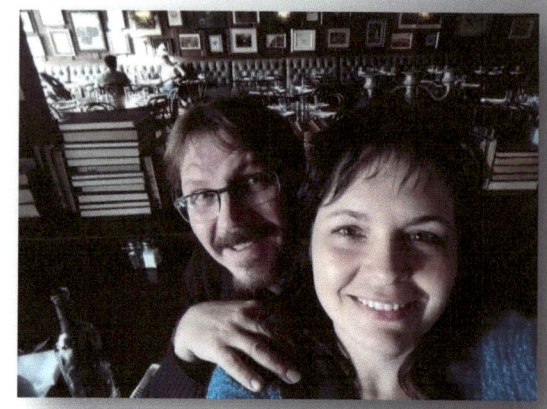

Lance Smith, Singer /Songwriter/ Artist/ Servant

Lance has dedicated his life to reach his community with the love of Jesus Christ using the gifts God gave him. He has spent his entire adult life preaching the gospel of Christ and of His Kingdom in churches, street corners, alleys, public squares, parades, coffeehouses, yacht clubs, mountain tops, beachfronts and many other public arenas.

Lance and Annette Smith

You can find Lance singing in prisons, jails, nursing homes, hospitals, orphanages on radio, television, You Tube and concert venues around the world.

Lance has also drawn and sculpted Children's curriculum for the Assemblies of God and Pentecostal Church of God for 7 years. Commercial Sculptures by Lance can be seen in the Smithsonian, Grizzly Tools, Toy Story Land, Disney, Dollywood, Beverly Hills, Hollywood, Nashville, Universities Cabalas, and Bass Pro shops all over America and Canada.

More recently, Lance has added documentary filmmaking of the Holy land. In the last 10 years he has filled in At the IMAX Little Opry theater for James Garrett by Performing the "John Denver Tribute" in Branson Missouri. Lance has taken the John Denver show and morphed it to reach secular venues by adding an emphasis on the Creator not just the creation John loved so much. Lance is the father of five, three children of his own, Savanna Howland, Whitney Burgess, Adam Smith, and Step daughters Sierra and Shiann Adams. Currently Lance resides in Willard Missouri with his wife Annette, two step daughters Sierra, Shiann and grandson Jace.
Annette Smith

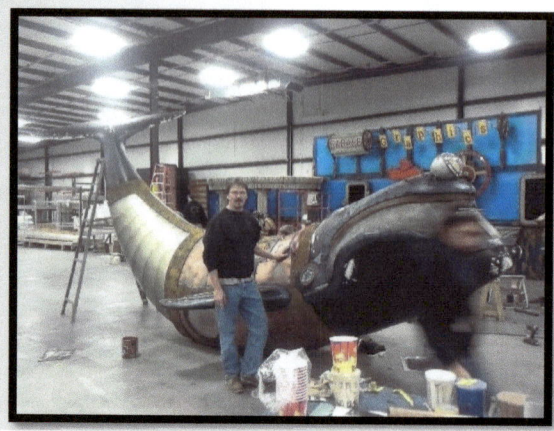

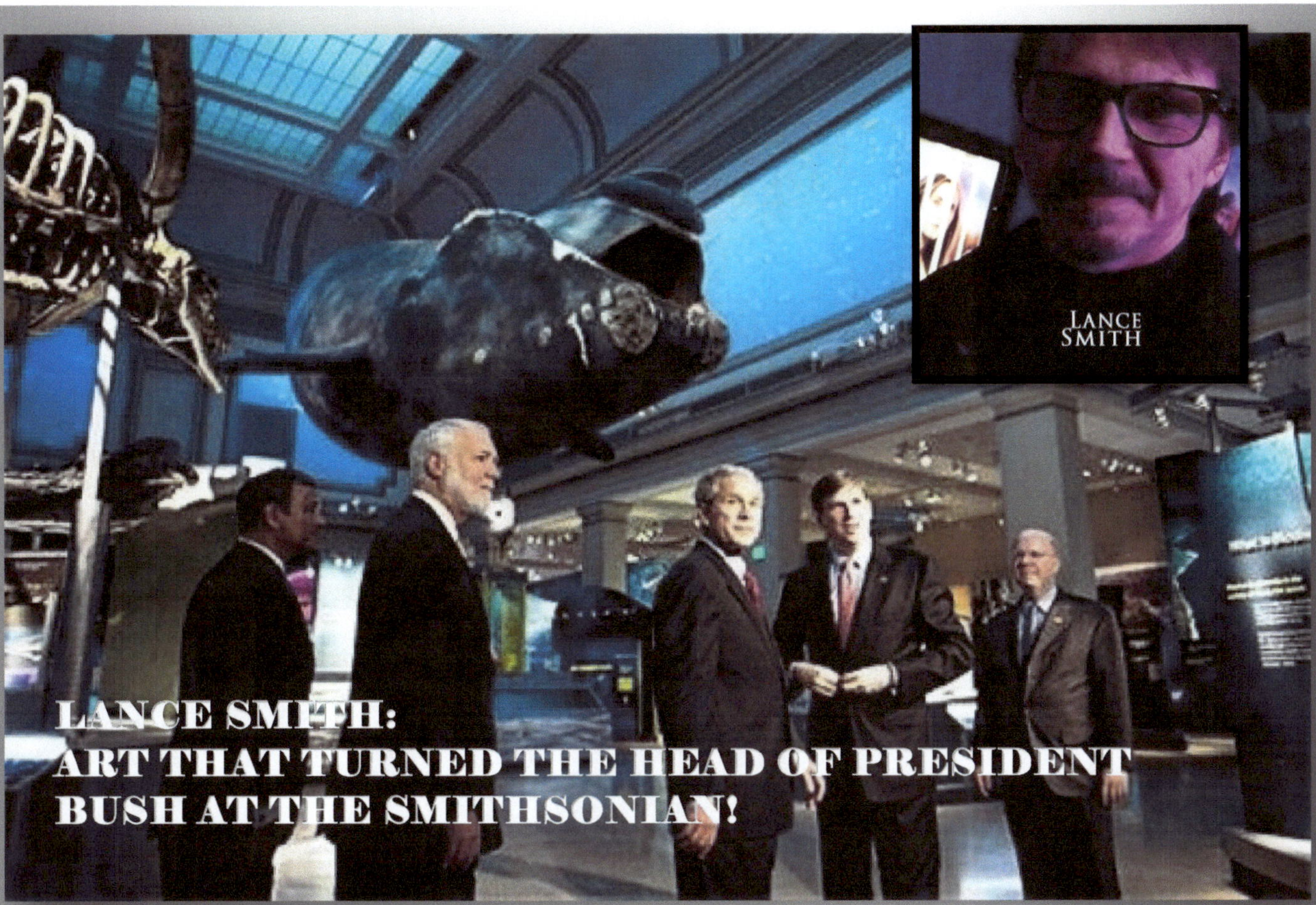

LANCE SMITH:
ART THAT TURNED THE HEAD OF PRESIDENT BUSH AT THE SMITHSONIAN!

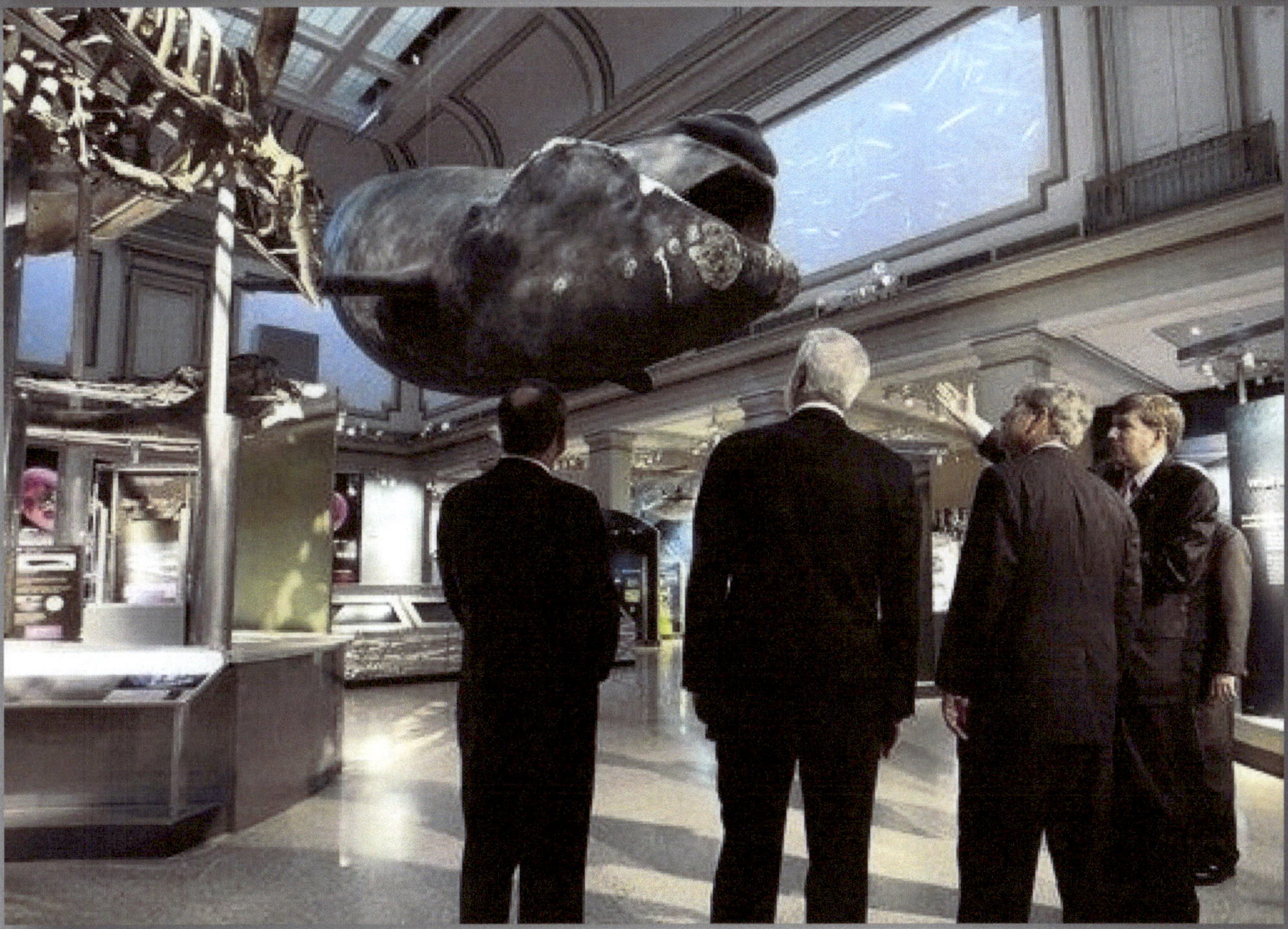

LANCE SMITH

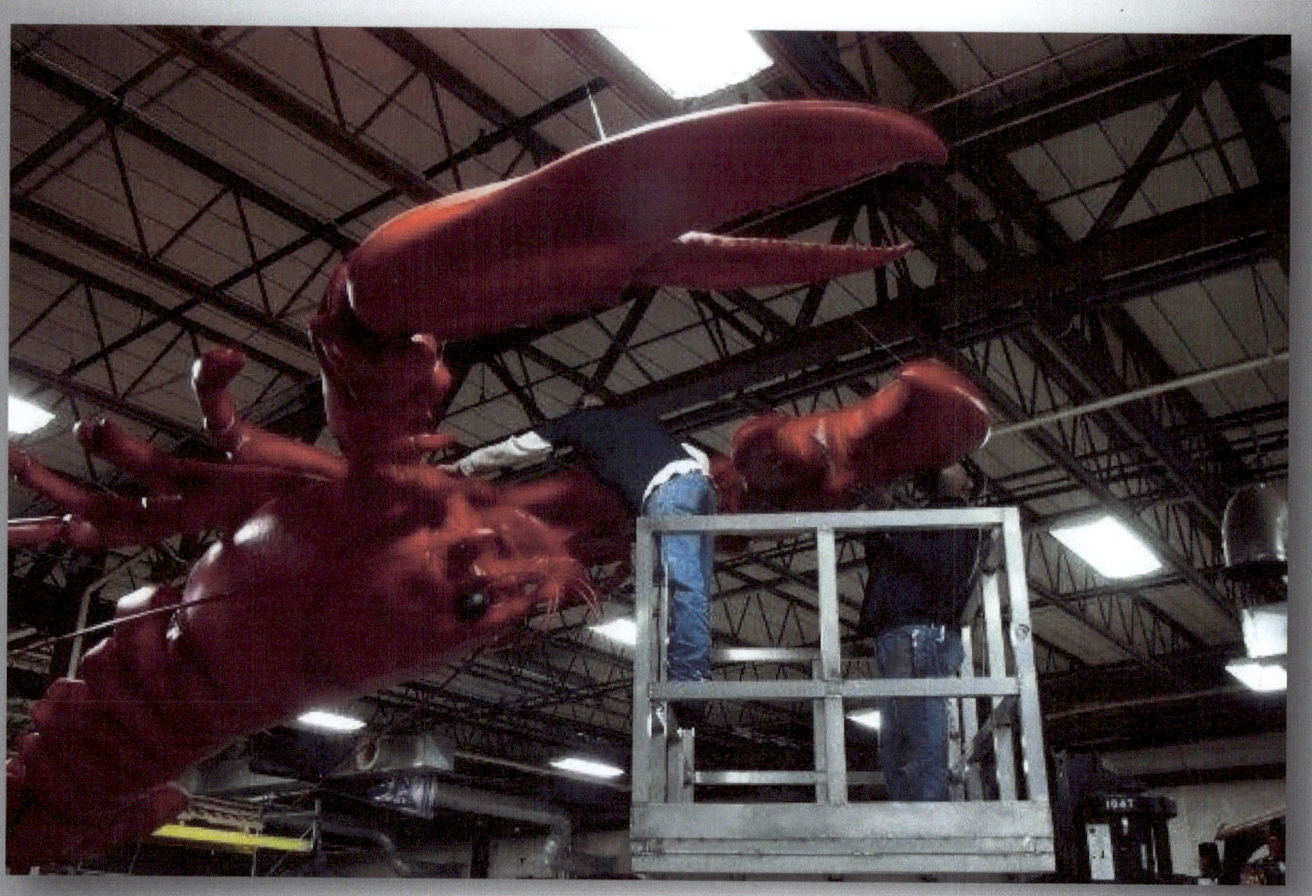

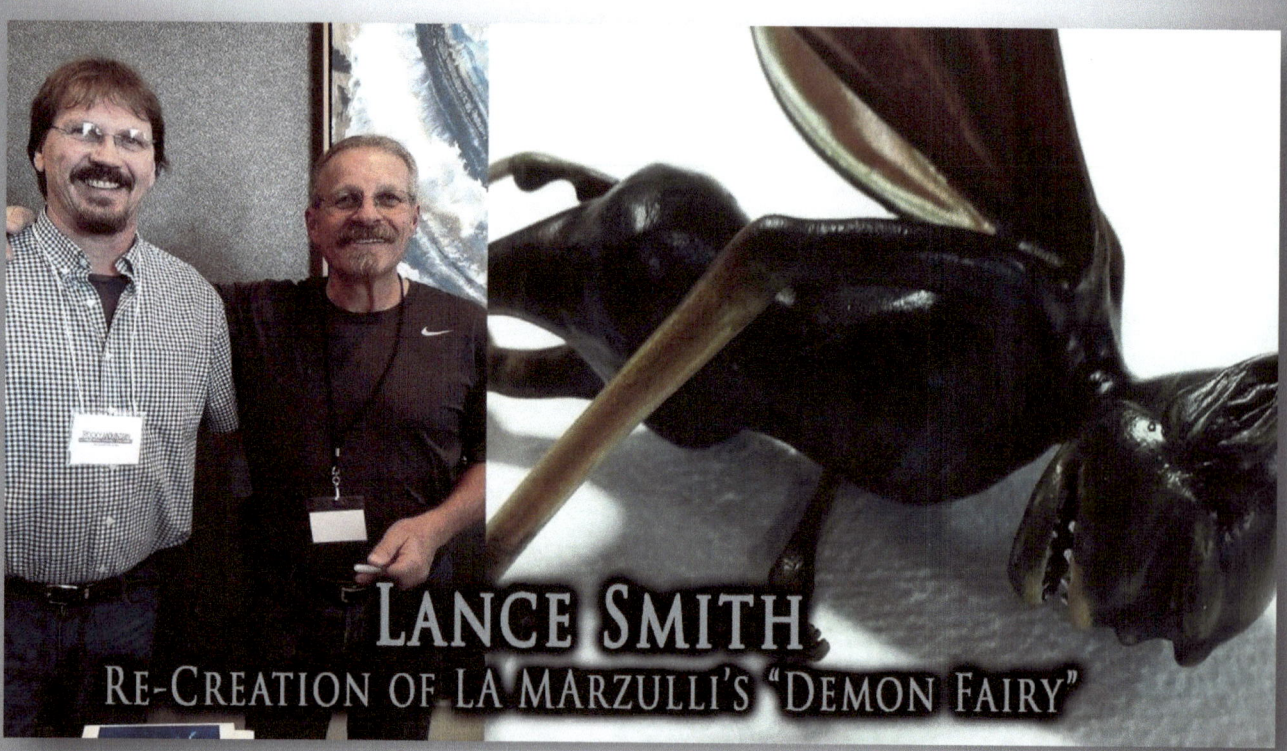

LANCE SMITH
RE-CREATION OF LA MARZULLI'S "DEMON FAIRY"

Talent is Cheap, but Dedication is Costly!

by: Lance Smith

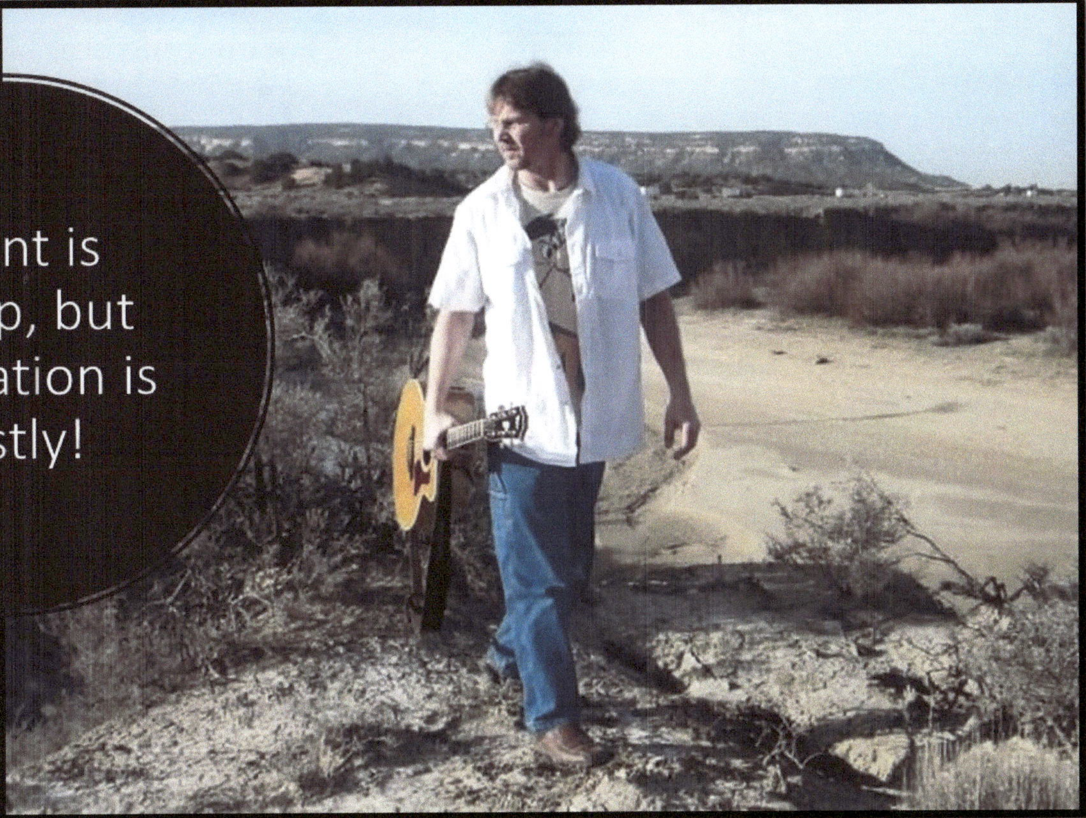

> Proverbs 18:16 "A man's gift maketh room for him, and bringeth him before great men."

Over the years I have had the privilege of meeting many people while in my role as a Youth / Worship Pastor. These folks have spoken to me about their various successes. They were from all walks of life, including singers, authors, speakers, mainstream musicians, politicians, pastors, evangelists, sports personalities, artists, even actors. Many are of unusual ability, who have spoken to me about their successes as well as their failures. All of them, without exception, are amazed at the journey they have been on and how they got to where they are now. The moment of reveal is always those most unforgettable moments they find themselves filing in the folder of life achievements. Singers, gaining opportunities to sing in front of Presidents, Speakers filling stadiums with their finest orations, Painters finding their works hanging in the palaces of kings, and Sculptors smiling as they see their works hanging from the rafters of the Smithsonian.

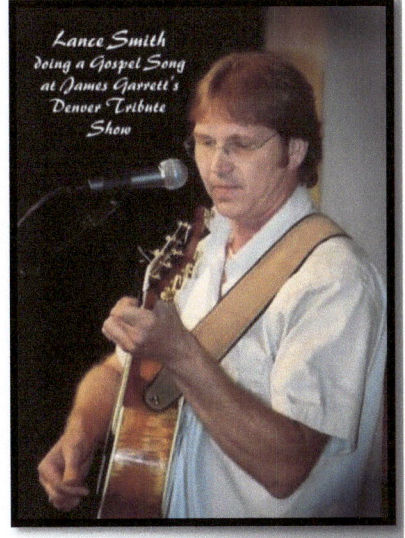

Lance Smith doing a Gospel Song at James Garrett's Denver Tribute Show

What these all have in common is a special seed of inspiration and ability the scripture calls talents/gifts. The Bible has a lot to say about talents/gifts. Proverbs 1:16 states that a man's gifts will make room for him and bring him before great men. I know that to be true, I can truly say I am a living example of a young man that did not think he had much to offer back to God. Sometimes the task we are faced with is to discover what our gifts are and how to develop them. It may be evident soon after birth or developed in its early stages by our environment. But I am convinced that we all have talents instilled in us by our creator. Jeremiah was told by the Lord, "Before I formed you in your mother's womb I knew you, before you were born I set you apart; I appointed you as a prophet to the nations." (Jeremiah 1:5) Think about it. We were somewhere with God before we were born into this life and our whole existence has been designed by the Great Creator. He has personally selected what gifts we will need to accomplish His will and placed them in us like an unopened package. What follows is a small snippet of my own story. So how does one get from a mind full of fear and confusion to one of Confidence in God? I am glad you asked.

We who were brought up in the church have all been raised with an admonition found in Proverbs 22: 6 which teaches us to "Train up a child in the way he should go: and when he is old he will not depart from it." And we have loosely been taught that this scripture means, take your child to church and Sunday school and when they get on their own they will be faithful to church. Actually, the scripture is better served if we include the context of the scripture around it. The Key to the passage is to Dedicate bring their gifting to maturity to fulfill their potentiality. In other words, when you dedicate the potentiality of a child, their talents/gifts to the Lord, you as the parent now are in the position to allow God himself to develop and train your child for his service according to the talents and gifts our Father has placed in them. When anyone man, woman, or child is dedicated to service, God has promised to develop that person, place a call upon that person, fill that person with the power of the Holy Ghost, and to Guide that person into success for the kingdom. Being in Church is the simple manifestation of that dedication. His gifts and calling are without repentance. Romans 11:29 tells us gifts once given to men from heaven are never taken back. His calling is extending an invitation to His people to partake in His favor and working in the kingdom. That is important because not only are we admonished to preach Jesus and Him crucified but to also preach the Kingdom of God and how we fit into it.

I remember struggling with that call. I was shy and awkward. I did not feel like I had much to offer anyone. I was 16 years old. I had been raised in a split home with a drinking father with a Spirit filled mother and 16 years of her fervent prayer and teaching under my belt. We moved to Missouri to a new environment and with new challenges. Brother Bill Hanshew was our Youth pastor in the little church in Springfield in the later part of the 70s. A man we greatly respected and admired. A man full of talent and dedication who squeezed every drop out of his gifts. I found a spot of comfort in the youth group to hide from my shyness, but I was just about to be discovered. And was inducted into Gods army.

The young Bill Hanshew was so fervent to his calling and would preach like his hair was on fire.. He started a youth choir that had a Holy Spirit fire lit under it. Those youth experienced spiritual insight they had never seen before. What I saw when I first attended there was just what I needed. I felt something I wanted, and God in His mercy had me right where he wanted me.

Six months earlier while living in central Idaho I had made a commitment and come to a resolution. I had asked the father to take my shyness and fill me with his Spirit. My former Pastor Don Shover had brought me so far. Taught me so much. He had poured into me knowing my own father was gone a lot. But moving to Missouri was a new life a new beginning and another man to speak into my life. Before I left I took 3 days to fast and pray. I drove to Lick Creek Summit east of McCall Idaho in the Sawtooth mountain range. A mountain 8089 ft. tall a mountain full of danger and intrigue. I conquered the mountain. At the summit of that beautiful mountain paradise, God met me in a life transforming way. My path had begun. I was saved many years before, but had I not been, this experience would have sealed the deal. At the summit among the huge granite boulders I read about Moses and his mountain experience and the question YHVH asked Him, pounded in my ear. "What do you have in your hand" We all Know it was his Shepherd's rod. God used it throughout his life to perform His miracles. It was a focal point in dealing with Pharaoh and His own people, the Hebrews. With it he was Striking rocks and splitting seas. I knew God was asking me the same question through that ancient text. "Lance what is in your hand?" At that point in my life I only knew of 2 things. A Guitar and a paint brush. I learned early what my giftings were and I absolutely loved them, even screamed out for a chance to use them. I figured if God gave them to me I needed to dedicate them to Him which I did. I did not realize then the more you use them for God the more he would add to your gift box. But what else I learned from that mountain experience was Moses became great when he became a servant. Putting God first, others second, and yourself last. I now understand some people struggle a little bit longer to discover their gifting but at that point I was a little naïve. And my wall that blocked my success was an incredible shyness. Well, I came down off the mountain, but do not believe for a moment I was in the valley! I knew it was time to step out in faith and see what happened. Talent is cheap, but dedication is costly.

Faith was intact, raw talent was there. But without dedication it went nowhere. 1 Samuel 16:16 says, "Let our lord now command your servants, which are before you, to seek out a man, who is a cunning player on a harp; and it came to pass, when the evil spirit from God is upon you, that he shall play with his hand and you shall be well." Notice the word cunning! Cunningness provided an effect; it drove the evil spirit out. Psalms 33:2 says, "Praise the lord with Harp: sing to Him with the psaltery and an instrument of 10 strings. Sing to Him a new song; play skillfully with a loud noise." This instruction from The Lord to King Saul was to secure a man who could play skillfully. So what I learned from a young age was God uses dedicated people who would play cunningly and skillfully before Him. How interesting. God supplies the talent/gift, but you provide the dedication to sharpen that talent into a skillful instrument for his service. Wow! This thing is not about us at all! It is about Him! Very important thing to know in spiritual warfare is that our battle is not against flesh and blood, and we do not fight with carnal weapons. My fear was about to be destroyed.

Immediately I began to pray and purify my heart. Then I dedicated myself to practice, practice, practice. If I am going to do spiritual warfare or encourage the body of Christ, I wanted to do it skillfully. Not to glorify myself, but to glorify God. I think one confusion that I see young people struggling with in our society is really cognitive dissonance. They want to be famous, an American Idol. It seems to be about fame, fortune, and bling. But take heed, the five "I will's" found in Isaiah 14 that caused Lucifer to fall, reflects a heart of pride and Idolatry. A real confusion among the youth is that the church needs to imitate the world in order to be relevant. You know, I have learned that we should never offer God an inferior or corrupted sacrifice. He is worthy of more. The best of our talent, zeal, heart, and spirit, with NO compromise. If God transforms us into a new creation, then let Him create something in you that is fresh, innovative, and of Heaven's culture. Something bigger than you or what society says you should be.

At 16, I began to visit the Nursing Homes taking my guitar with me, singing and praying for the older folks. I figured if they could not roll away fast enough in their wheel chairs I had a readymade audience. I was right! Those were the early seeds that eventually choked out on shyness and inferiority mindset. Without realizing it,

God was helping me put on the Mind of Christ and take off the mind of fear. And the music took care of itself.

So earlier I mentioned my youth pastor, Bill Hanshew, God bless him. His philosophy was to do it with a love for God and have fun while doing it. He created a space where we could learn, with platform where the youth could minister. Nursing homes, Youth rallys, camps any number of outreaches was where I cut my teeth on my early ministry. It was invaluable training that he made fun. I have to say without him speaking into my life I may not have crawled out of my shell, took a risk, or dedicated my gifts.

I read a historical story once that really helped me. Few people outside of the art culture have probably heard of this story. A Famous man, an artist named Bertoldo de Giovanni, was the pupil of the greatest sculptor of his time Danatello. He grabbed the baton and became a great sculptor himself, in his later life he was commissioned to teach a young man by the name of Michelangelo. Michelangelo at the age of 14 began to learn from Bertoldo who was quite impressed by the raw talent and effortless skill of the teenager. One afternoon as Bertoldo walked through the classroom he witnessed young Michelangelo haphazardly chipping away at an expensive piece of marble. The young man with apathy and laziness performed with a careless attitude that infuriated Bertoldo. The master grabbed the hammer out of Michelangelo's hand and to his utter surprise smashed the sculptor and pulverized it into dust. Grabbling the young man's shoulders, he shouted, "Michelangelo! Talent is cheap! But dedication is costly!"

For years now, I have worked in the arts. God has been so good to me. I have sung in concert halls and theaters. I have met so many famous and talented people. Always consider- ing it a great honor. I have produced sculptors that have been on Television shows. I have sculpted large museum pieces that hang in the Smithsonian. Sang and played guitar all over the world. His Blessings are abundant, my heart is so fulfilled. I have had opportunities few have had...but seriously without direction and a purpose, talent is cheap, Bertoldo was right. God is the dedication, his purpose in me is not to make me great, but to reflect His greatness. Not to make me famous but to make me holy. One last thing I need to say.

If you are good at something you do not need to inform the world about it, they will see it. Your focus should be excellence. But if you want to be great, learn to be a servant. So, let us say you are really good at something. Let us say people really like what you do and are always complimenting you. What do you do? How should we respond? It is very simple; say:

1. "Thank you!" That is it! Simply say, "thank you!" The rule of thumb in etiquette is short. I appreciate your kind words or that is kind of you. By accepting the compliment, you show your gratitude.

2. Share the compliment. If you accomplish something as a team, acknowledge the compliment by saying "Thank you, I will pass on your kind words to my team." It is a wonderful opportunity to speak into someone else's life by edifying them and acknowledging their contribution.

3. Be mindful of your nonverbal behavior. Watch your body language as you accept a compliment. Pay close attention to your posture. Make eye contact. Lean forward slightly. Avoid closing yourself off by crossing your arms. Above all else smile.

4. Avoid compliment battles and false humility. That means creating an excuse of how poorly you did in order to elicit more compliments.

God desires us to be the best we can be. Not by comparing your talent or gifting with someone else. The body of Christ is very unique and different. False humility is really pride poking its ugly head up for a word of flattery. Remember "pride goes before destruction and a haughty spirit before a fall." Proverbs 16:18.

I recall reading a story about Holocaust survivor Cory Ten boom, daughter of a Dutch watchmaker in the 1940s. At a Christian conference she related her amazing story of survival at the Auschwitz concentration camp and the loss of her family in the prison camps of WWII. At the end of her presentation on forgiveness the crowd erupted in thunderous applause and a standing ovation that took 3 minutes to subside. When the last

hand clap ended, she raised her head to look at the crowd. Wiping the tears and memories from her eyes she stated: "I take your roses and lay them at the feet of Jesus." Wow! What a humble servant of God! Would that we all could take our flower and crowns and lay them at the feet of Jesus.

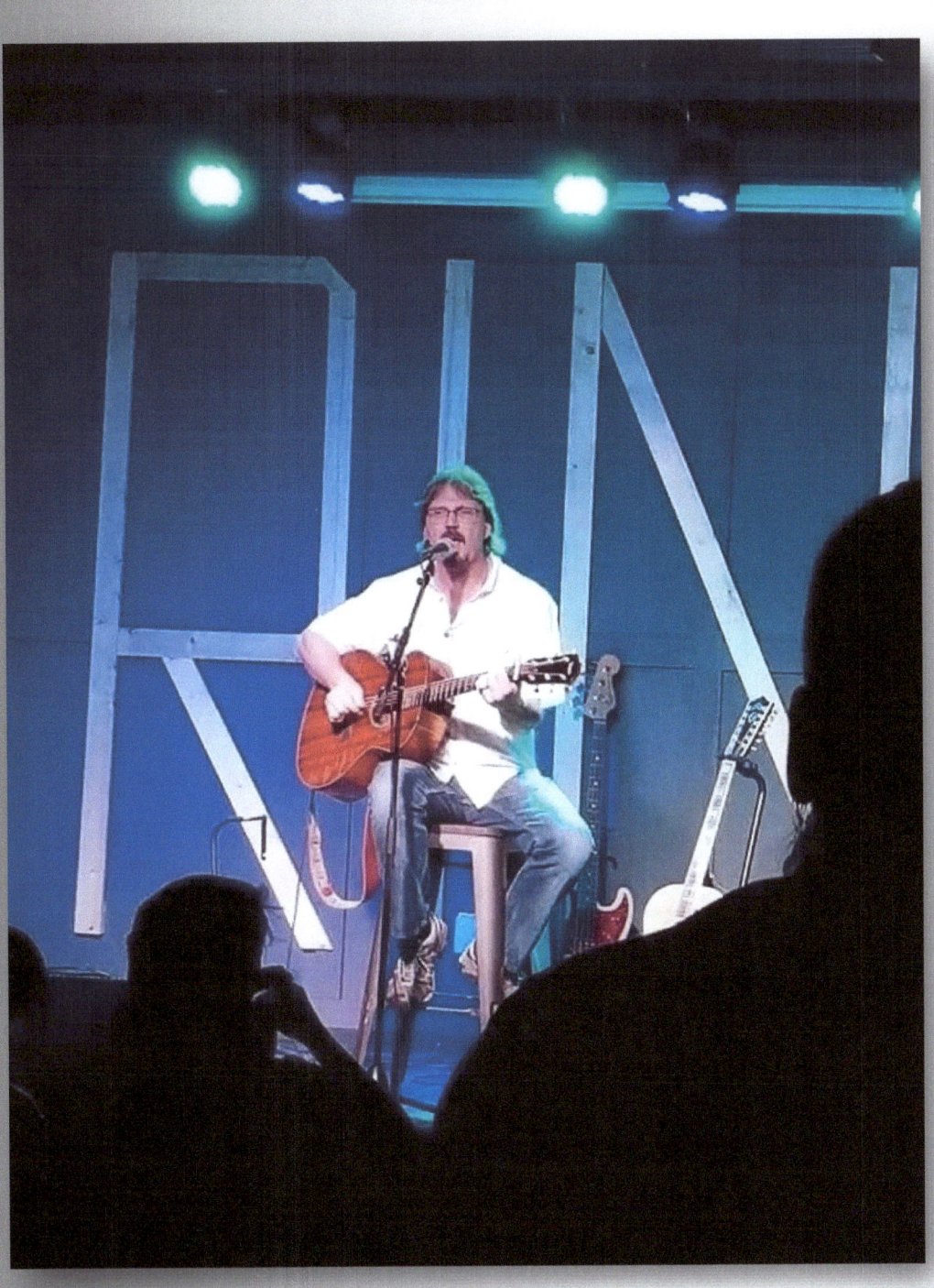

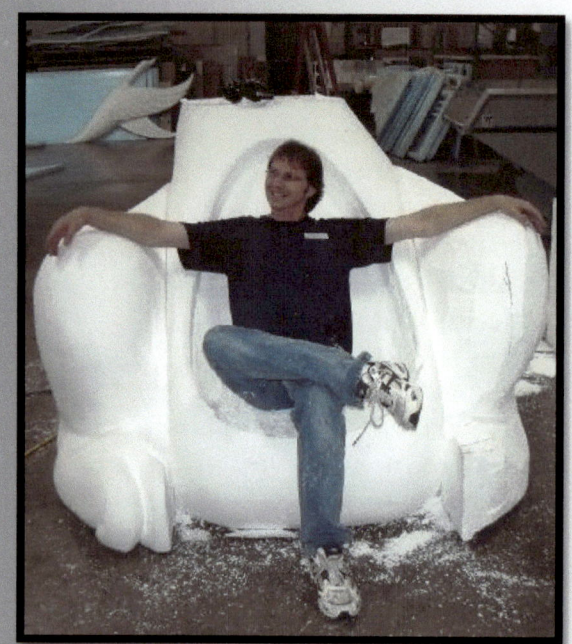
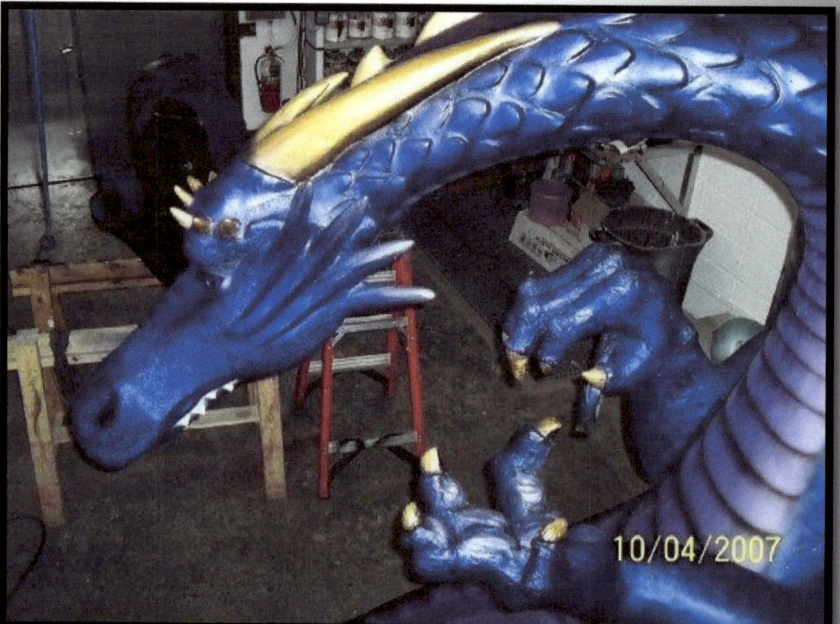
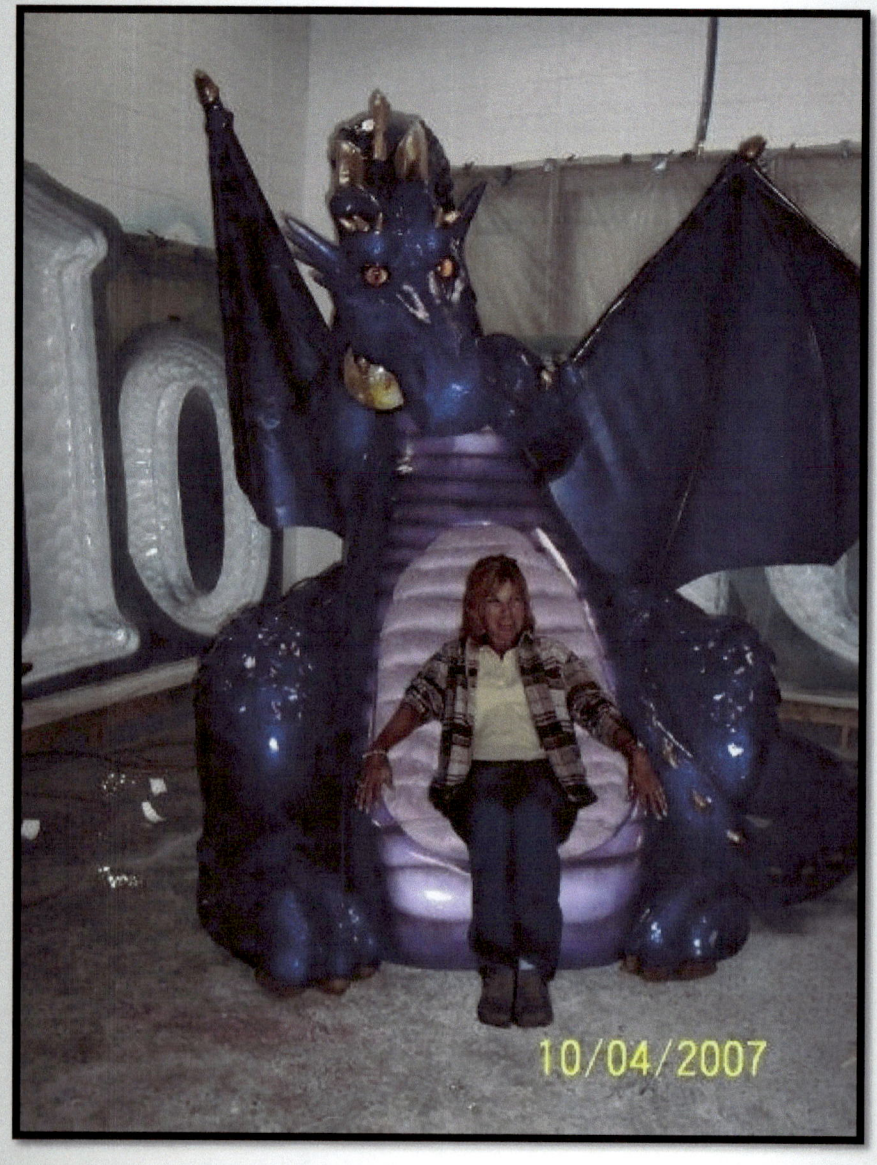

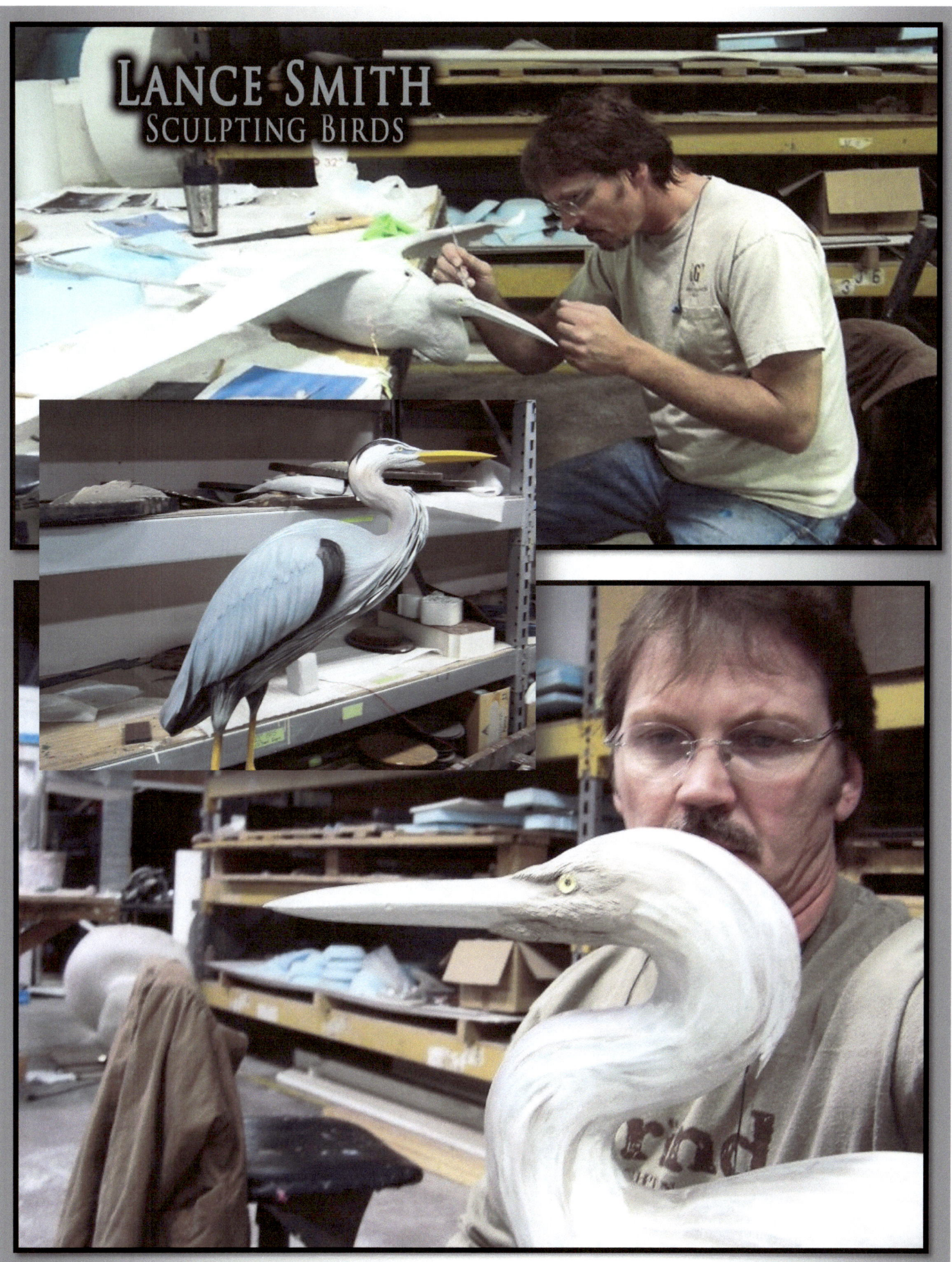

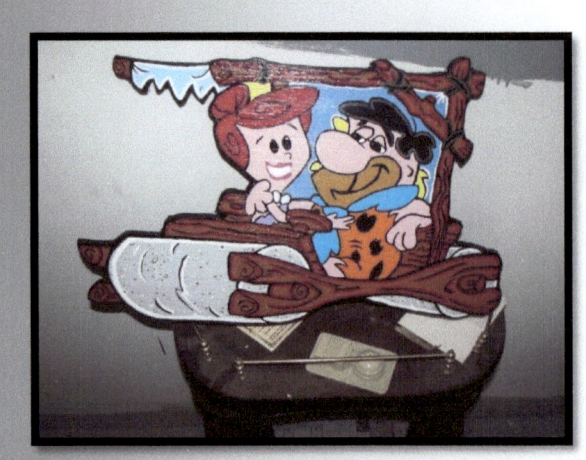
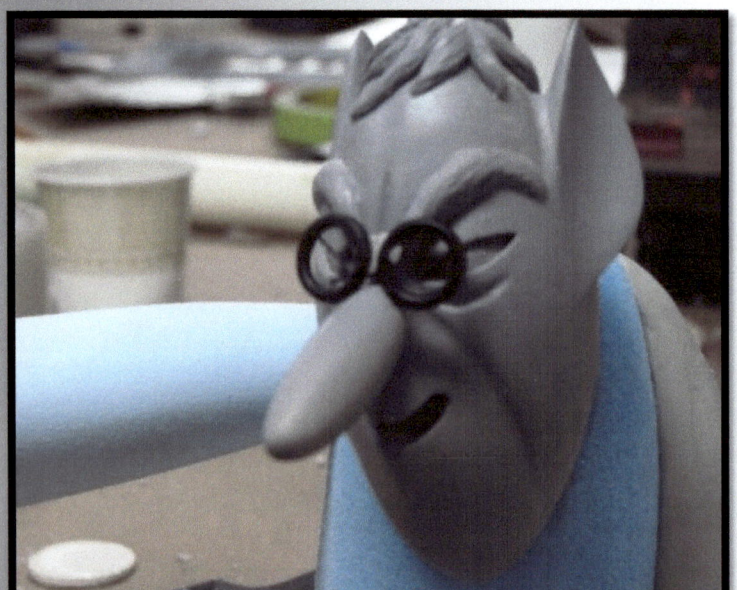
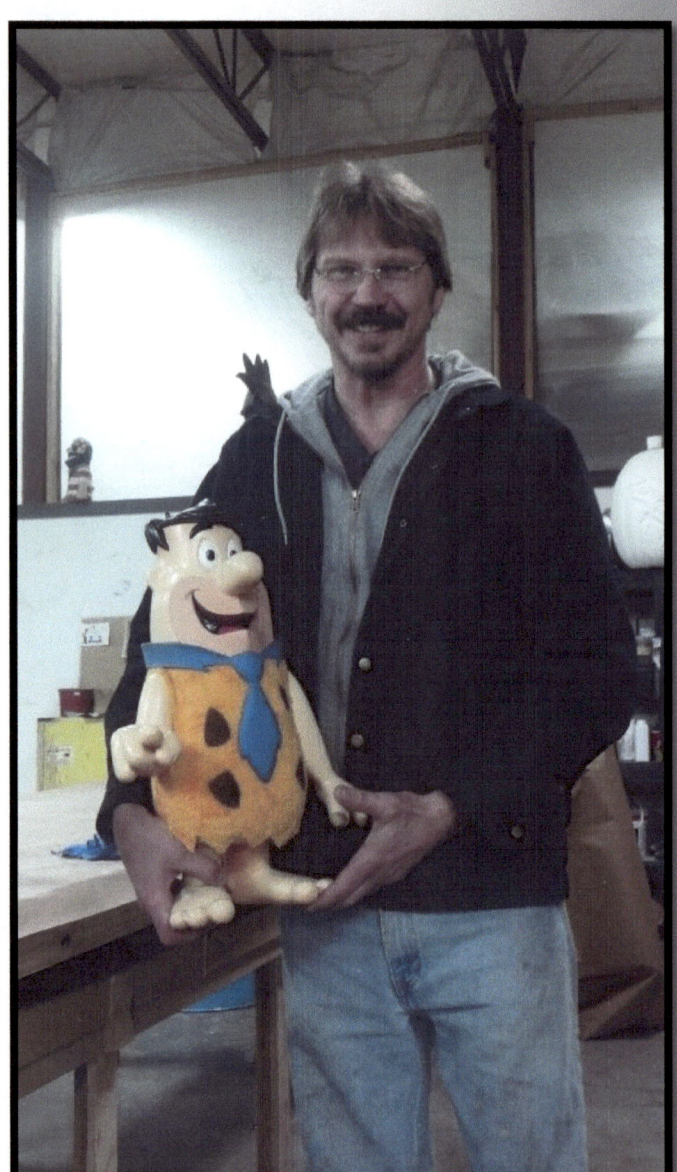
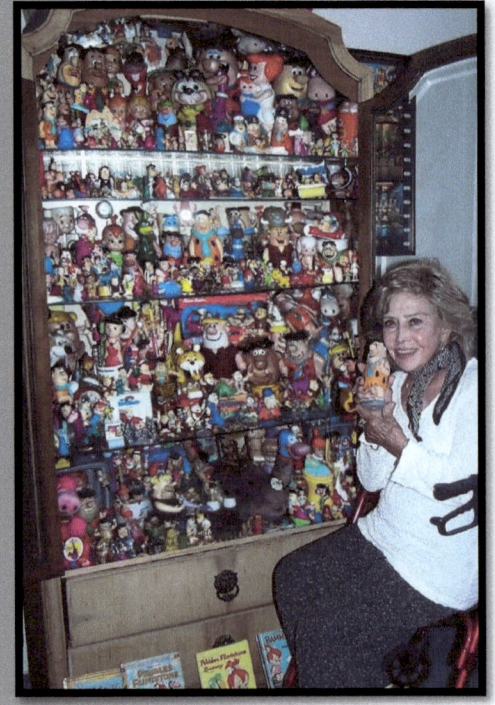
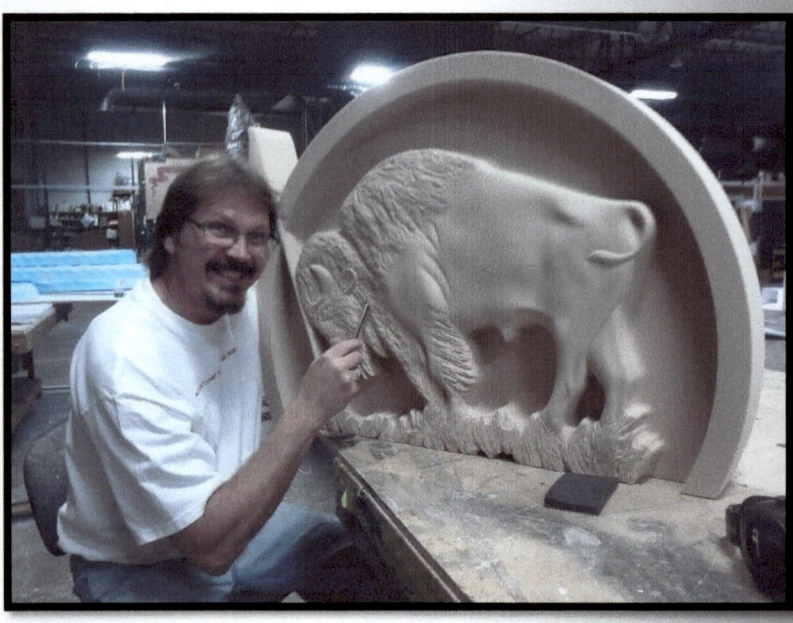

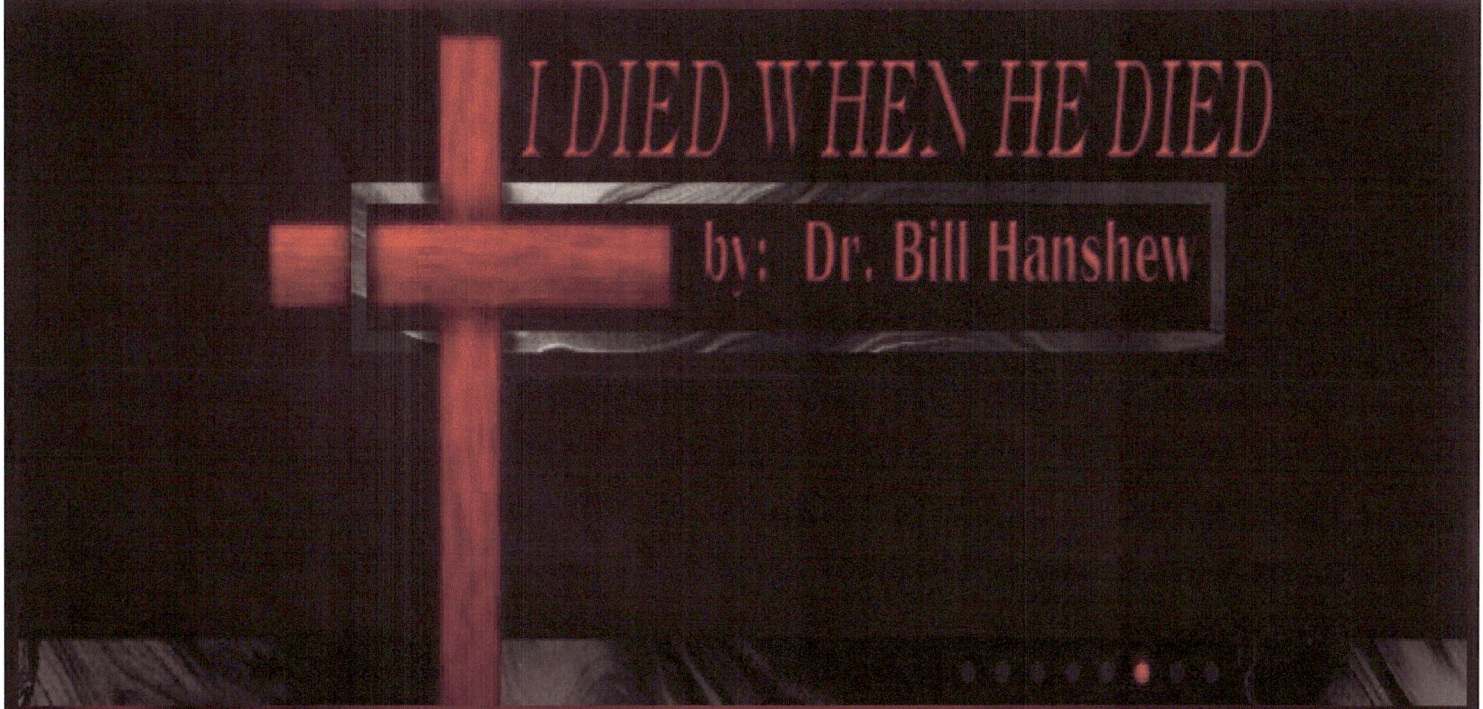

I DIED WHEN HE DIED
by: Dr. Bill Hanshew

Galatians 2:20 "I have been crucified with Christ; it is no longer I who live, but Christ lives in me; and the *life* which I now live in the flesh I live by faith in the Son of God, who loved me and gave Himself for me."

Just to recap, the Apostle Paul, formerly named Saul was a persecutor of Christians. He was not known for being a nice guy. Acts 8:3 says, "As for Saul, he made havoc of the church, entering every house, and dragging off men and women, committing *them* to prison."

But one day, on the road to Damascus, while Saul was still threatening followers of Jesus, he had an encounter with the Lord Himself. In Acts chapter 9, Saul heard the Lord speak to him and he said, "Who are You, Lord?" And the Lord said, "I am Jesus, whom you are persecuting." Saul had an encounter with Jesus that day.

Now, some say it was approximately 15 years after Saul's conversion that he wrote what was recorded in the book of Galatians. This is when the renamed Saul makes this statement in Galatians 2:20, "I have been crucified with Christ; it is no longer I who live, but Christ lives in me; and the *life* which I now live in the flesh I live by faith in the Son of God, who loved me and gave Himself for me." I think that literally Christ's death became Paul's death.

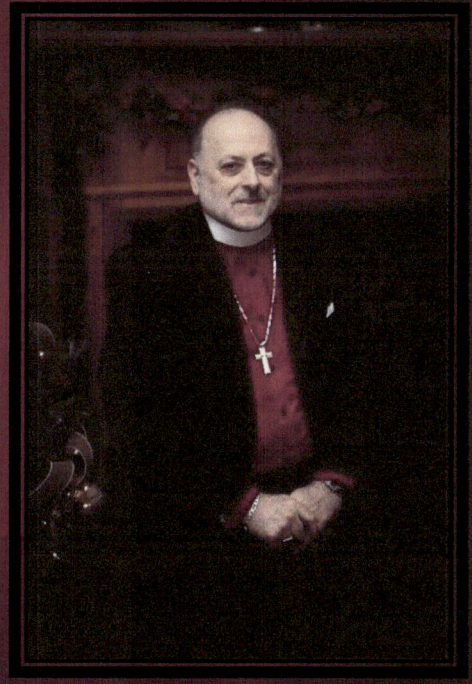

What Paul says previously in this same chapter is that he identifies himself as a Jew and states that "We Jews know that we have no advantage of birth over "non-Jewish sinners." We know very well that we are not set right with God by rule-keeping {which speaks of the law} but only through personal faith in Jesus Christ." And he goes on to say in the Message Bible, "How do we know? We tried it—and we had the best system of rules the world has ever seen! Convinced that no human being can please God by self-improvement, we believed in Jesus as the Messiah so that we might be set right before God by trusting in the Messiah, not by trying to be good."

This is, in part, why I believe he came to the conclusion that when Christ died, the old nature of Paul also died. He said, "I have been crucified with Christ; it is no longer I who live, but Christ lives in me." Some people see themselves in their performance-based lives. If they do well, they see themselves as justified before their God. If they do poorly, they in turn see themselves as disapproved by the same God.

However, a person's performance, good or bad, can never declare a person righteous or non-righteous. Paul said in Galatians 2:19 (MSG) "I tried keeping rules and working my head off to please God, and it didn't work. So, I quit being a "law man" so that I could be *God's* man." Therefore, you and I must see our old performance-based nature as having died when Christ died. We must stop trying to base life as a Christian on whether we perform well or not.

Now that does not mean that Christians should not pray (as in communication with God) or study our Bibles (as in search out the truth), or faithfully attend a house of worship (as in having fellowship and spiritual nourishment), and to even give of our finances in support where the Holy Spirit leads us to give. It just means that how God sees you is not based on how well you carry out each task, but He sees you in the death and life of Jesus.

Galatians 2:20 (CJB) says, "When the Messiah was executed on the stake as a criminal, I was too; so that my proud ego no longer lives. But the Messiah lives in me, and the life I now live in my body I live by the same trusting faithfulness that the Son of God had, who loved me and gave himself up for me." As Jesus hung there on that cross, in a substitutionary sense, the whole world hung there in Him and with Him. It was the same as if you and I were hanging there. We were not beside Him, we were in Him as He held us in His heart.

Paul says from the Message Bible in Galatians 2:20 "Christ's life showed me how and enabled me to do it. I identified myself completely with him. Indeed, I have been crucified with Christ. My ego is no longer central. It is no longer important that I appear righteous before you or have your good opinion, and I am no longer driven to impress God. Christ lives in me. The life you see me living is not "mine," but it is lived by faith in the Son of God, who loved me and gave himself for me." And I think that is the key right there when Paul says, "My ego is no longer central."

Paul is not telling us that his physical life ended, but that all he was prior to Christ came to an end and that he no longer was bound by human will or ego which prompted him to prove his worth in life, one way or the other. Paul says, "the *life* which I now live in the flesh I live by faith in the Son of God, who loved me and gave Himself for me." Life for you must become all about the Christ in you, not about the man or woman on the outside of you.

Paul concludes by saying, "I am not going to go back on that. Is it not clear to you that to go back to that old rule-keeping, peer-pleasing religion would be an abandonment of everything personal and free in your relationship with God? I refuse to do that, to repudiate {or renounce} God's grace. If a living relationship with God could come by rule-keeping, then Christ died unnecessarily." (Galatians 2:21 MSG).

The bottom line is that no one can ever be declared righteous or even justified by doing the works of the law. We are all justified by faith in Jesus Christ, nothing more and nothing less. Even when you claim to have a covenant with God, just remember that the New Covenant is between the Father and Son, and you and I simply soak up all the benefits by being crucified with Christ.

The God's Word Translation says, "If we receive God's approval by obeying the laws in the Scriptures, then Christ's death was pointless." My encouragement today is for you to stop seeking God's approval, or even the approval of man. Start living in God's approval which came by Jesus Christ. ...Think about it!

CHRIST DIED SO THAT YOU COULD LIVE!

THE 1ST ANNIVERSARY

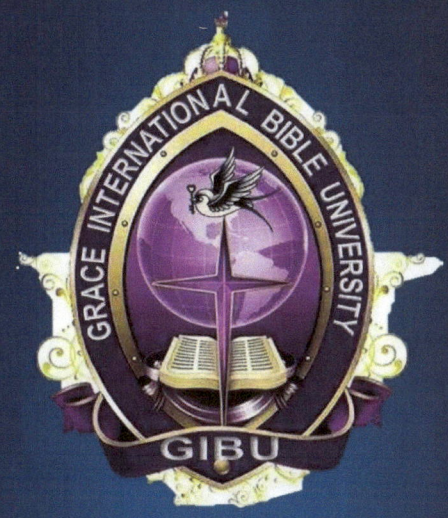

GRACE INTERNATIONAL BIBLE UNIVERSITY

2017 - 2018

Celebrating one year of accomplishment in Biblical Education!

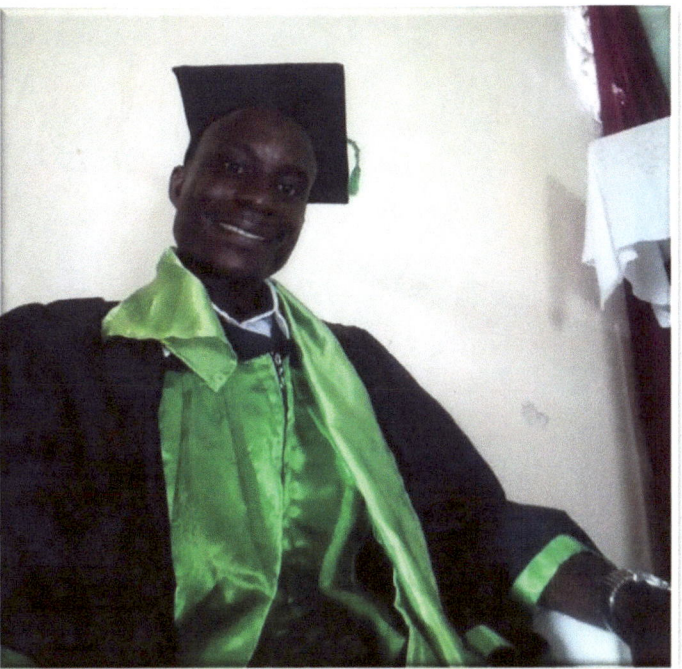

Dr. Rudolph Q. Kwanue, Sr.
Founder and Coordinator

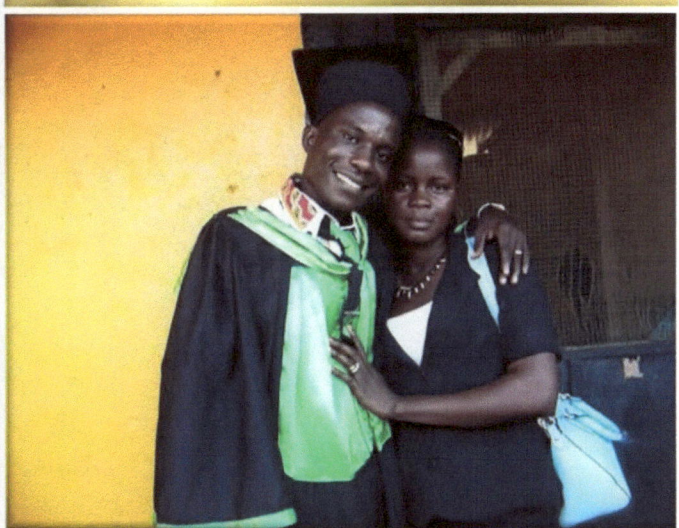

Dr. Rudolph Q. Kwanue, Sr.
and Mother Rita Kwanue

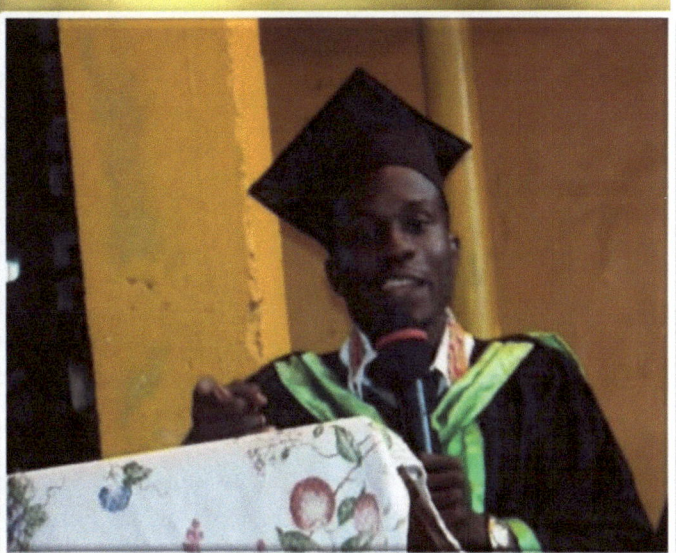

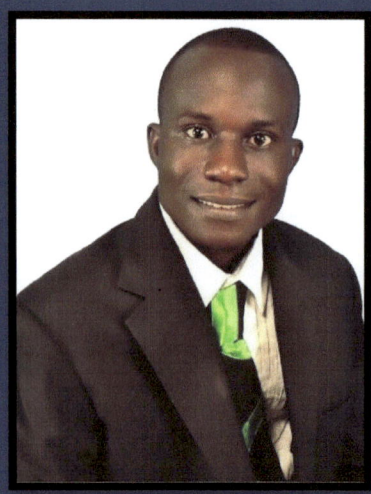

Rev. Dr. Rudolph Q. Kwanue
Founder and Coordinator – GIBU
Based in Liberia, Africa

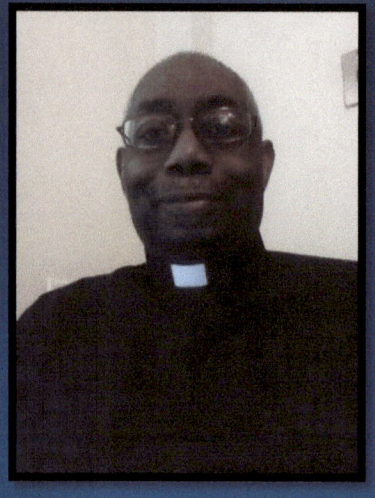

Bishop Dr. Frank A. Willett
International President – GIBU
Based in Pikesville, MD

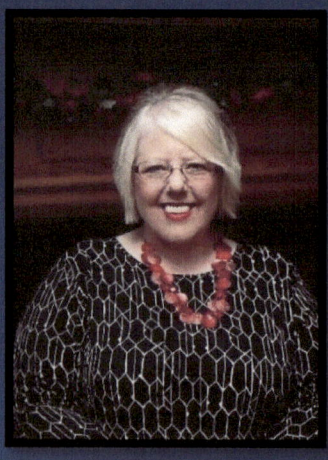

Dr. Faye Hanshew
Administrator and Graphics Designer - GIBU

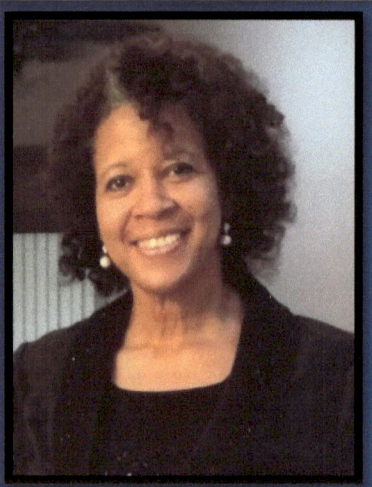

Dr. Maureen Whitehead
Position: International Consultant and Curriculum Specialist – GIBU
Based in Florida - USA

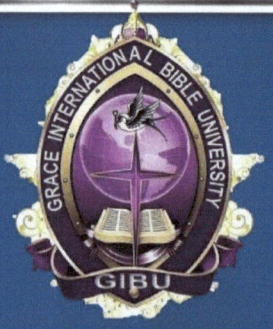

GIBU BOARD OF TRUSTEES

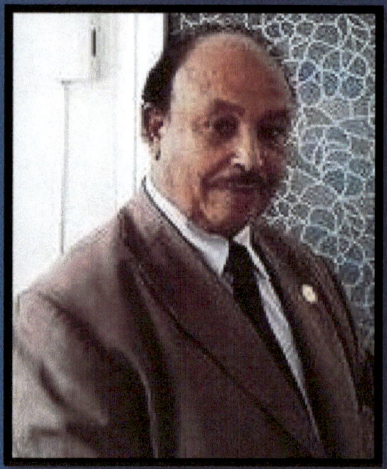

Bishop Dr. Yebiyo Ghebrezghi
International General Secretary and National Director
Based in Democratic Republic of Congo DRC

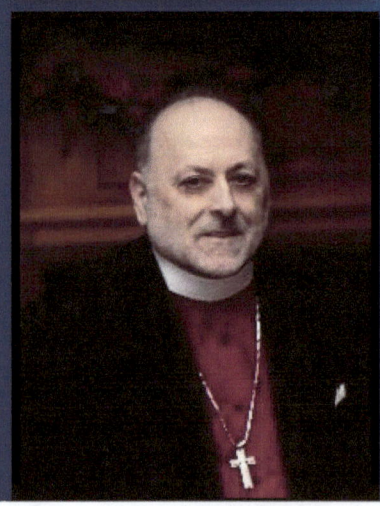

Bishop Dr. Bill Hanshew
International Consultant – GIBU
Based in Missouri - USA

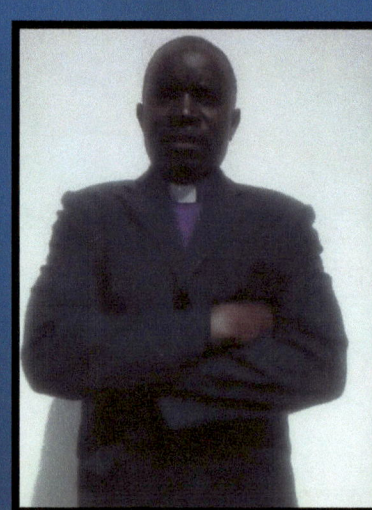

Bishop Dr. Fighton Chilufya
International Dean of Student and National Director - Zambia
Based in Zambia, Africa

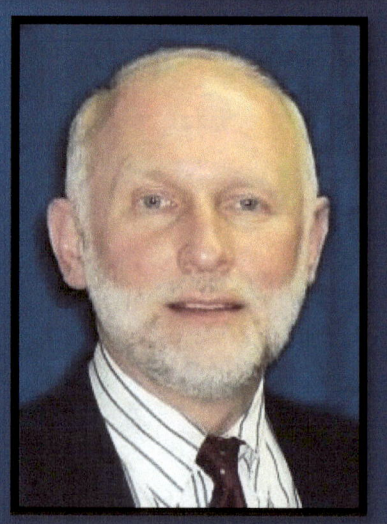

Bishop Timothy A. Johnson
International Senior Advisor – GIBU
Based in Minnesota - USA

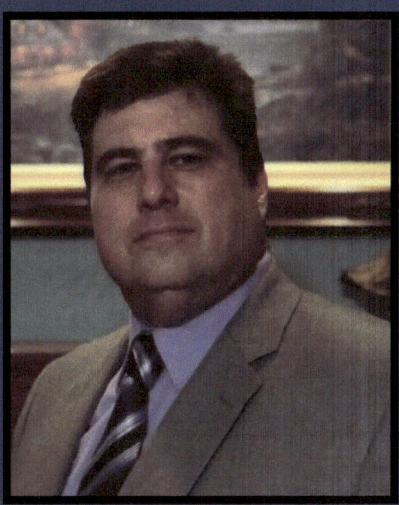

Dr. Glen Hartline
International Vice President – GIBU
Based in Louisiana - USA

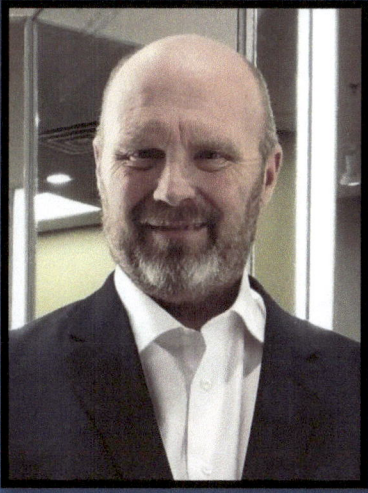

Bishop Benjamin Paris
International President – IACE
International Prayer Director - GIBU

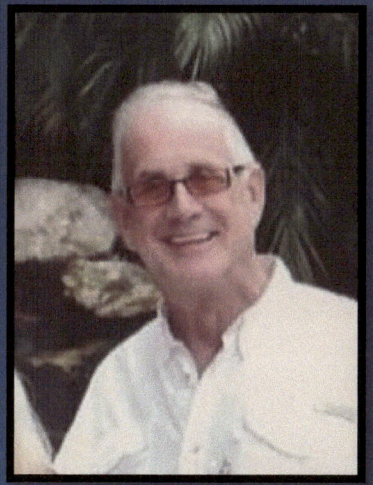

Rev. Ronnie Earl Tisdal
Director of Online Education - GIBU
IACE Agent – Florida - USA

OTHER MAJOR LEADERS

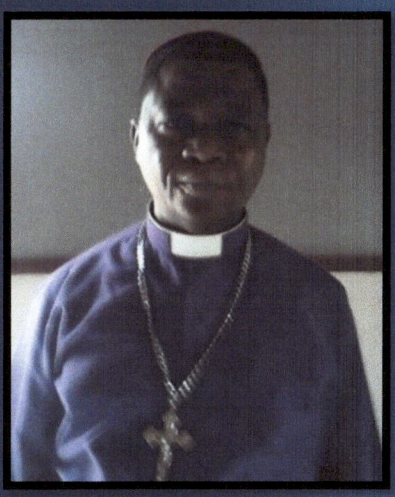

Bishop Dr. Daniel Ghansah
Director – Ghana – IACE

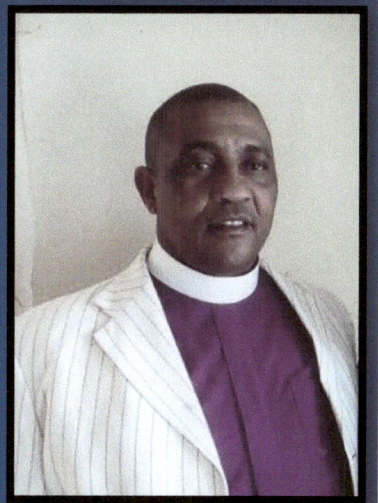

Bishop Dr. Michael Tshangela
Director – South Africa – IACE

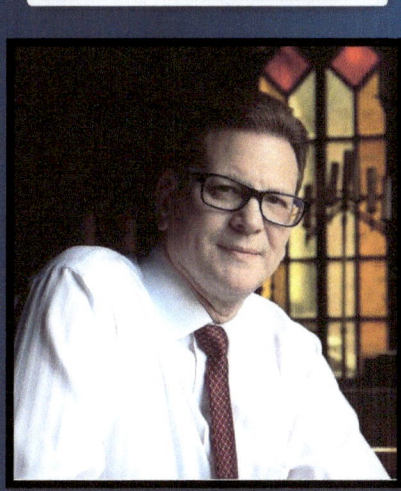

Rev. Dr. Charles J. Sathmary
Director – Canada – GIBU
International Vice President - IACS

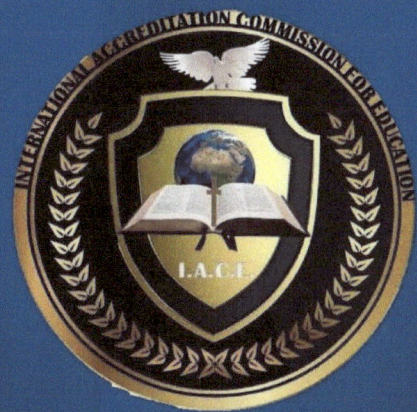

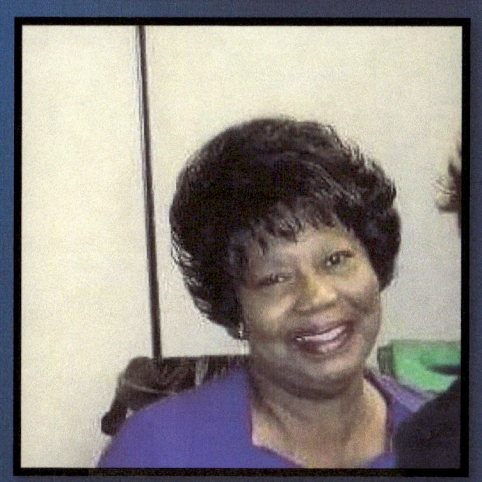

Dorline Jordan
Sponsor GMS - USA

NATIONAL LEADERS

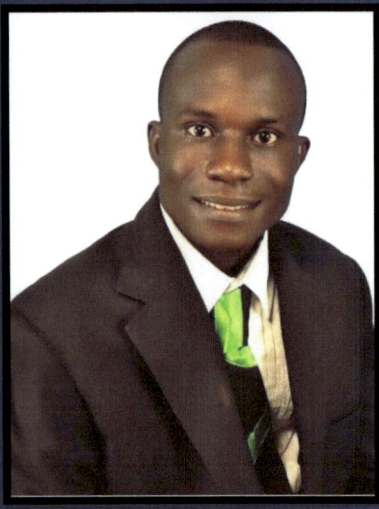

Rev. Dr. Rudolph Q. Kwanue Sr.
Position: National Director - The Republic of Liberia
Contacts:
Phone: +231-777-260-959/888-63-15-93
Email: rudolphkwanue@yaho.com
and Gracecollege578@gmail.com

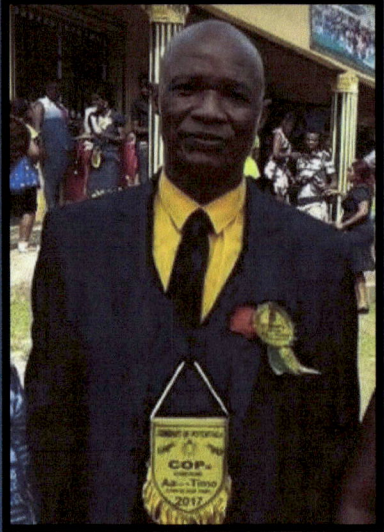

Rev. Wallace B. Kamara
Position: National Dean of Students - Liberia

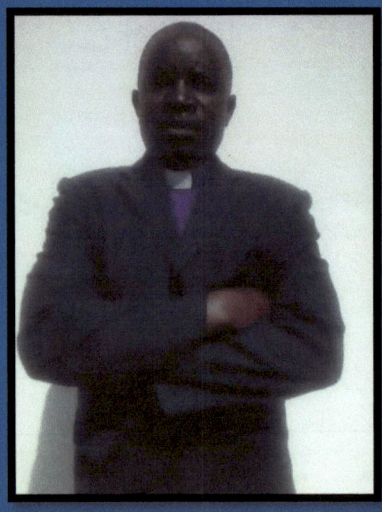

Bishop Dr. Fighton Chilufya
Position: International Dean, National Director - Zambia

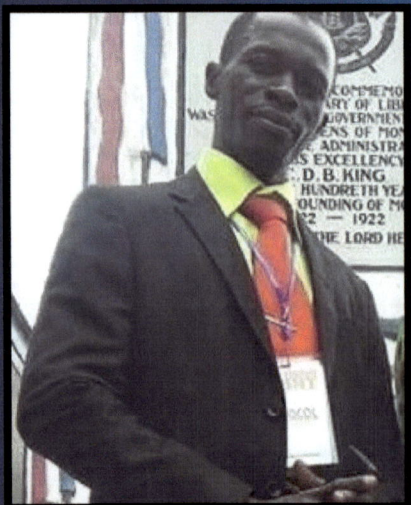

Rev. Trustine Lifted Momo
Position: National Coordinator - Liberia

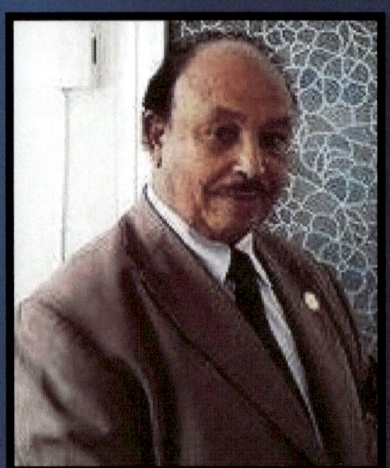

Bishop Dr. Yebiyo Ghebrezghi
Positions: National Director – Based in Democratic Republic of Congo DRC

AFRICAN DIRECTORS

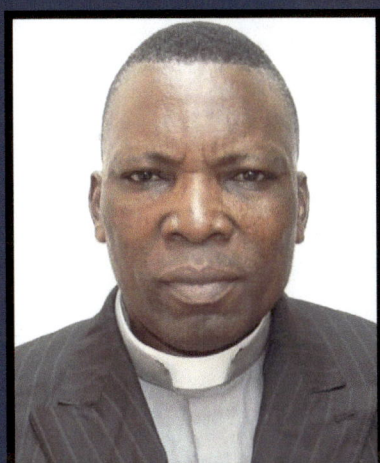

Bishop Dr. Pierre
Position: Director – Benin Republic

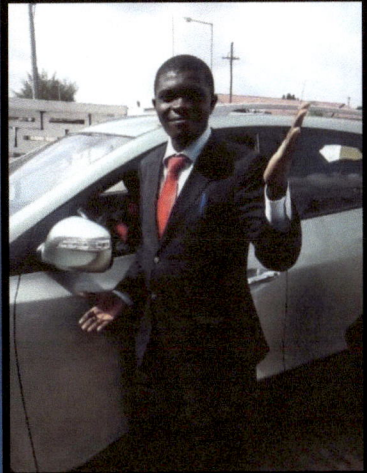

Rev. Alexander Tweneboah
Position: Director – Ghana

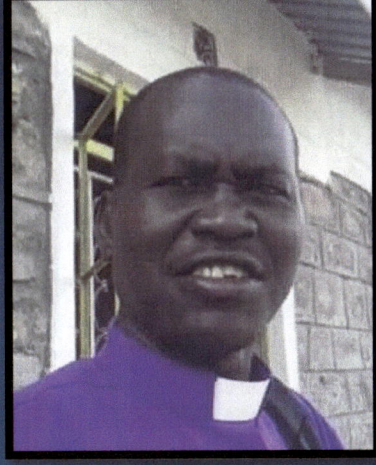

Bishop Dr. Jacob Ekutan Etheri
Position: Director – Kenya

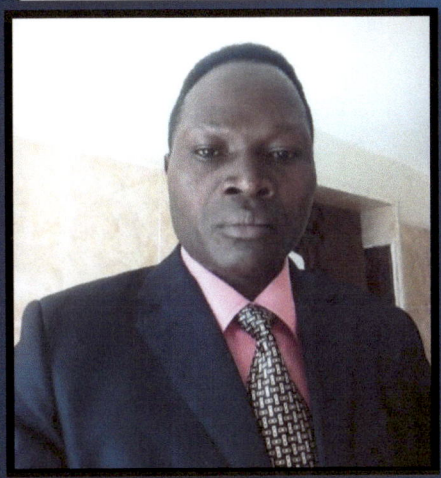

Bishop Isaiah Jackson
Position: Independent Director – Western Region – Kenya

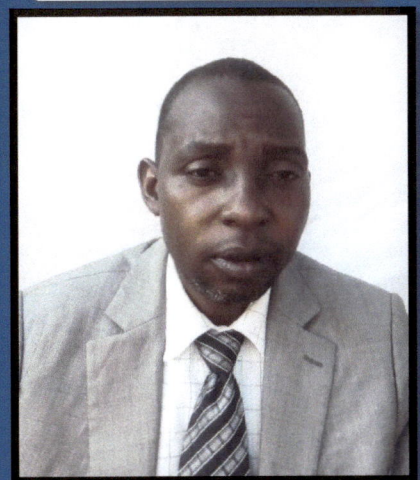

Bishop Patrick Jackson
Position: Director – Malawi

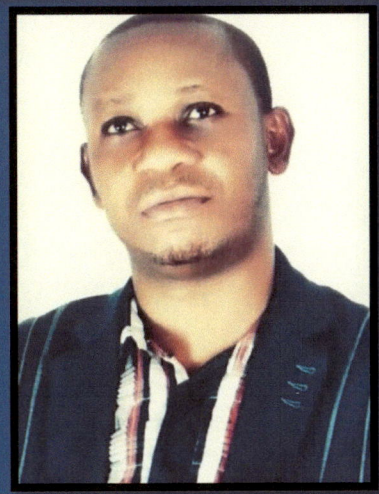

Rev. B. B. Felix
Position: Director – Nigeria

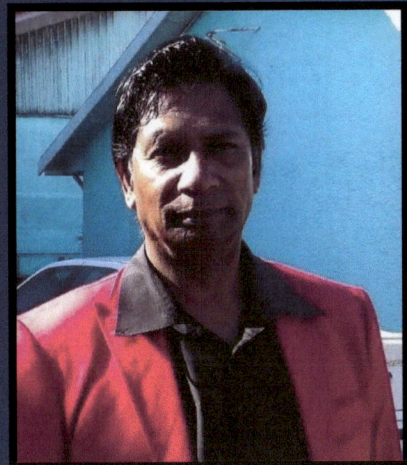

Rev. Dr. Wesley Puckree
Position: Director – South Africa

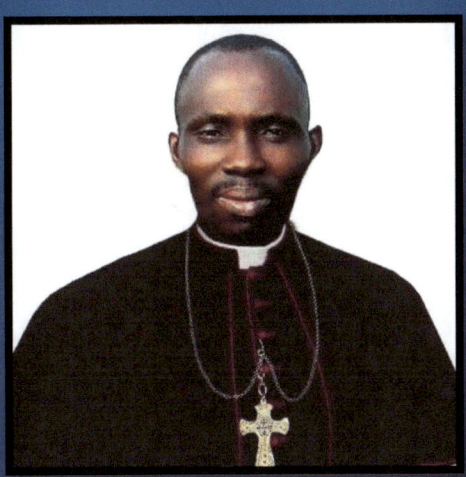

Bishop Dr. Stephen Kwabla Gbeve
Position: Director – Togo

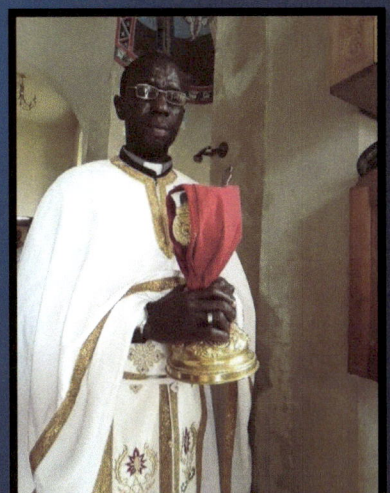

Rev. Elvis Aaron Fofanah
Position: Director – Sierra Leone

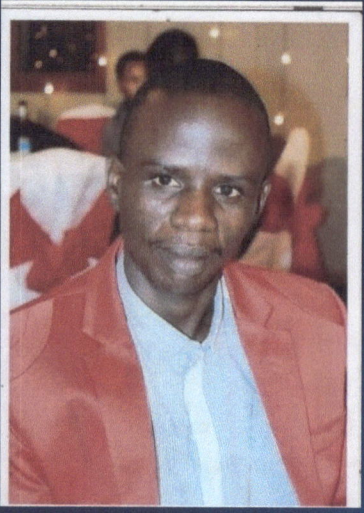
Bishop Ogechi Innocent
Position: Director – Liberia

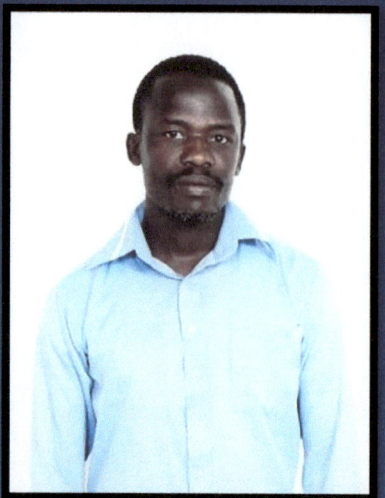
Apostle Dr. Bekhi Makhwe
Position: Director – Botswana

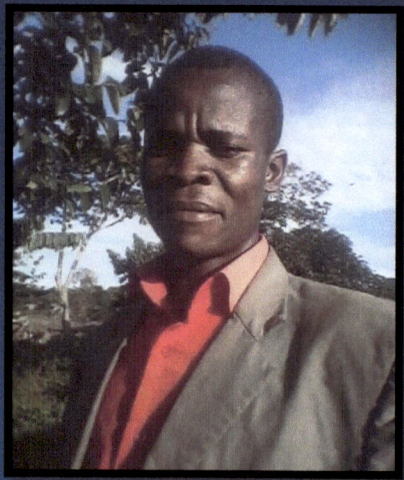
Rev. Wamalwa Benard
Position: Director – Uganda

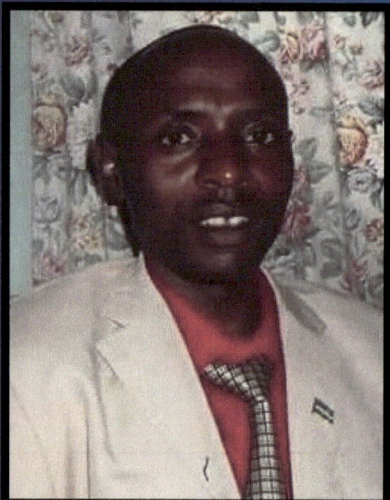
Apostle Dr. Nizeyimana Vedaste
Position: Director – Rwanda

GIBU DEPARTMENT HEADS

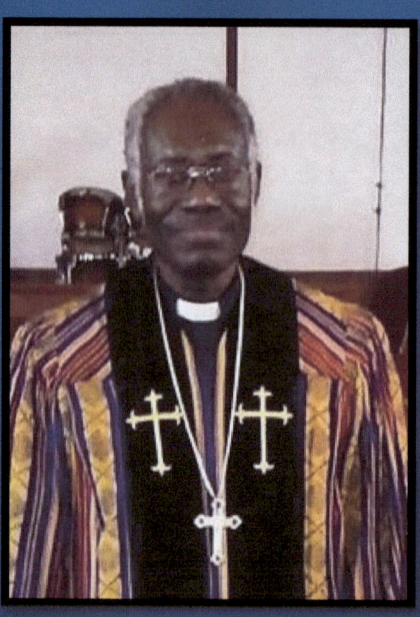
Bishop Dr. Emmanuel Osei
Theology Head – GIBU

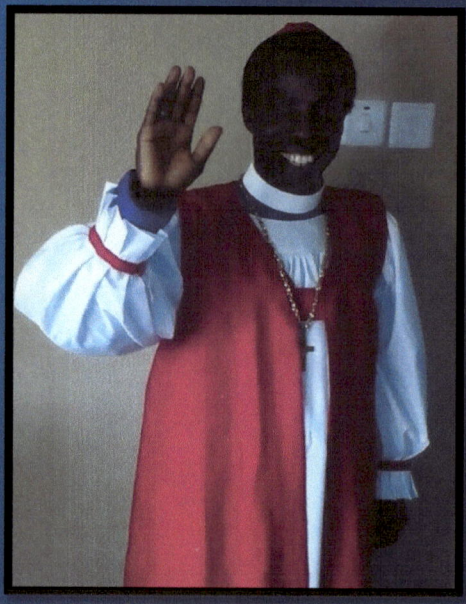
Bishop Dr. Daniel Ayo Deji
Homiletics Head – GIBU

AUSTRALIAN DIRECTOR

CANADIAN DIRECTOR

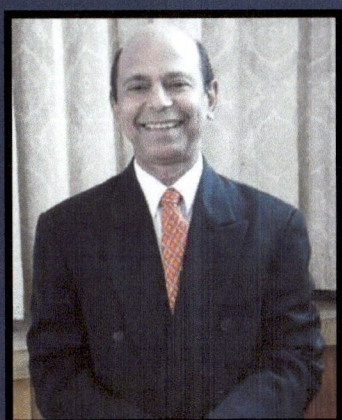

Rev. Dr. Amar Raj – Director
– Australia - GIBU

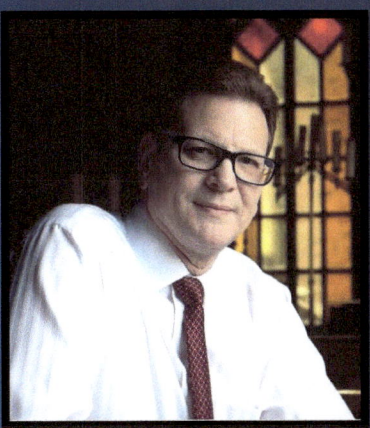

Rev. Dr. Charles J. Sathmary
Director – Canada – GIBU
International Vice President - IACS

UNITED ARAB EMIRATE DIRECTOR

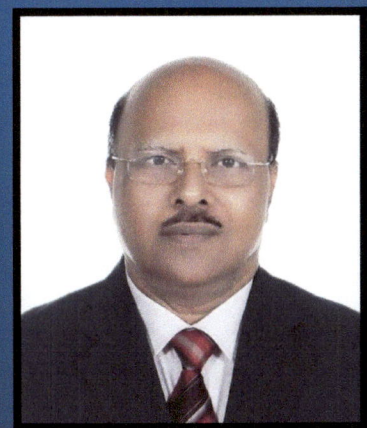

Apostle Dr. Anthony
Director – United Arab Emirate – GIBU

INDIAN DIRECTOR

USA DIRECTORS

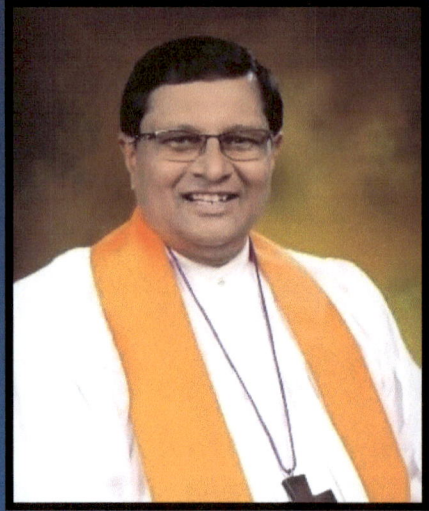

Rt. Rev. Dr. Pramod Goni
Position: Director – India

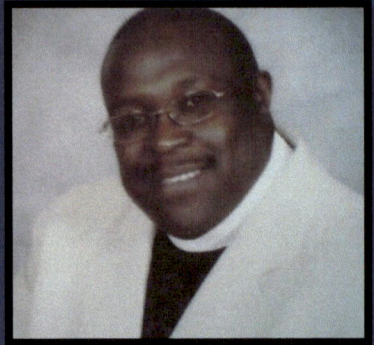

Bishop Dr. Eric Johnson
Position: Director - Georgia

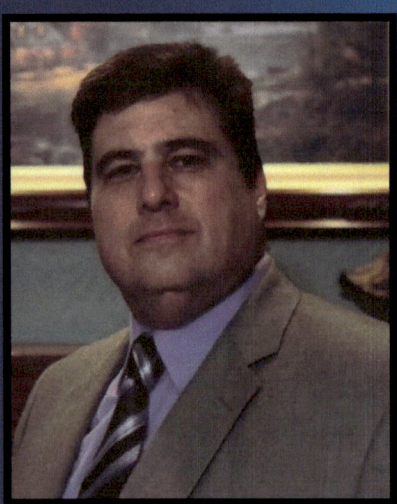

Dr. Glen Hartline
Positions: International Vice President – GIBU
Director - Louisiana - USA

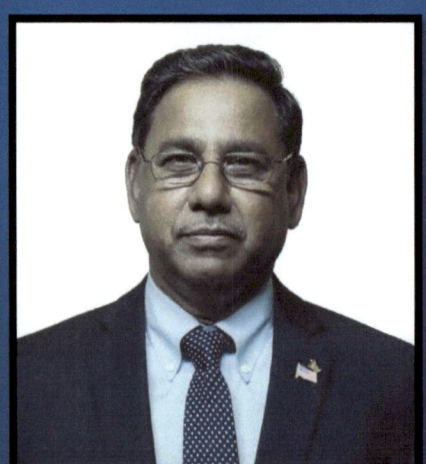

Bishop Dr. Emmanuel Irshad Masih
Position: Director - Pennsylvania

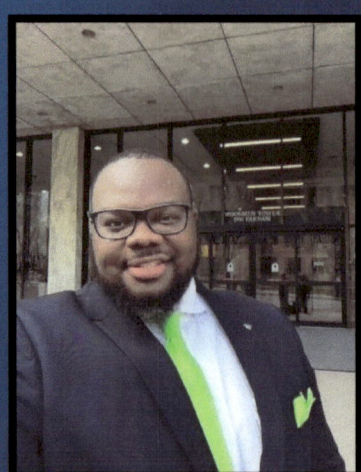

Bishop Dr. Laramie J. Jackson
Position: Director - Texas

ADVISORS

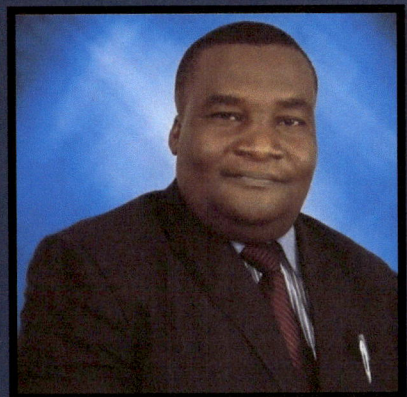

Bishop Josephert Bukachi
Position: Senior Advisor - Kenya

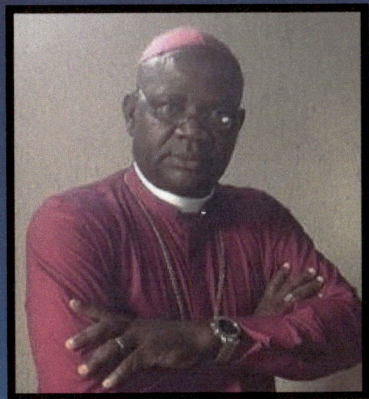

Bishop Dr. Nate Ezeh
Position: Senior Advisor – Nigeria
International French Translator

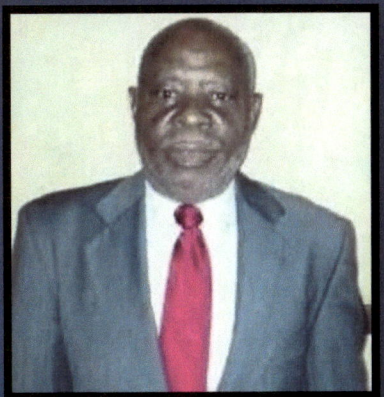

Bishop Steven D. Lewis
Senior Advisor – Liberia

Affiliate Schools and Universities

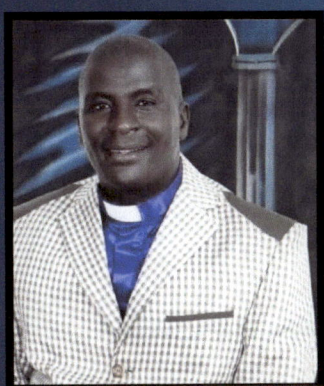

Bishop George Mogaka Momanyi
Position: Affiliate – Kisii, Kenya
(South eastern Kenya Region)

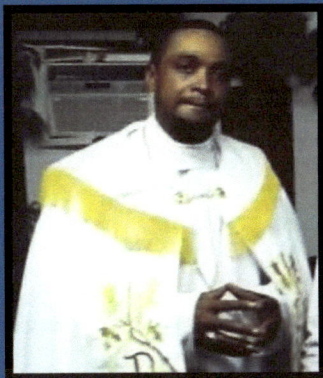

Bishop Elgin E. Blake
Position: Affiliate –
North Carolina - USA

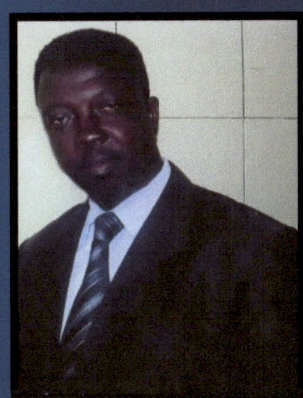

Apostle Victor Ogbonna
Position: Affiliate – Nigeria

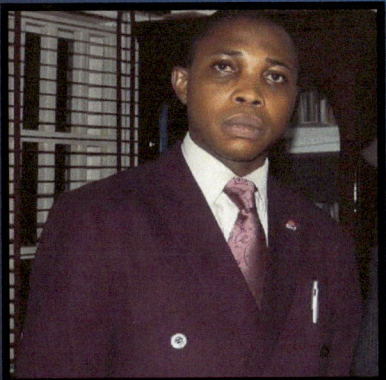

Bishop Dr. Osagie Success
Position: Affiliate – Nigeria

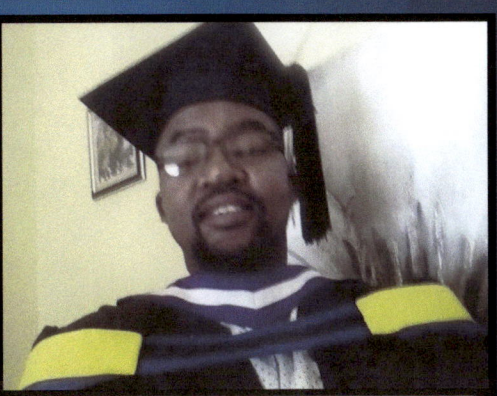

Bishop Dr. Thulani David Matambeka
Position: Affiliate – South Africa

ASSISTANT DIRECTORS

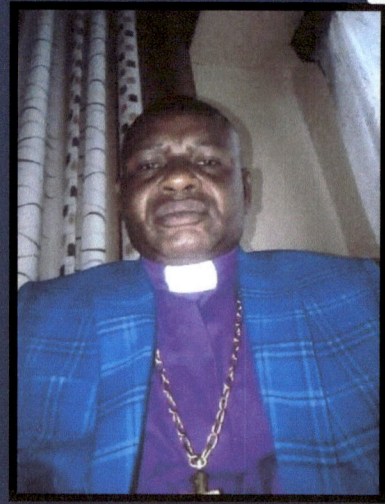

Bishop D. Dieudonne Ngombe
Position: Assistant Director - DRC

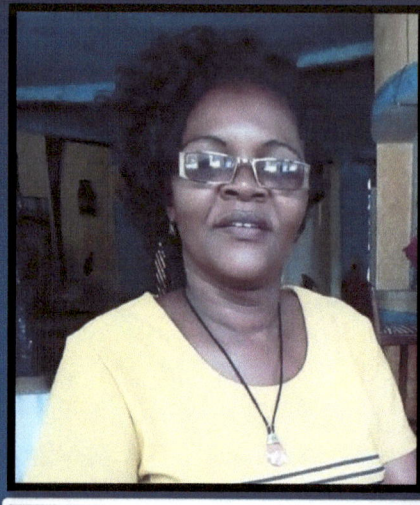

Bishop Dr. Priscillah Haburisa Nzaro
Position: Assistant Director - Kenya

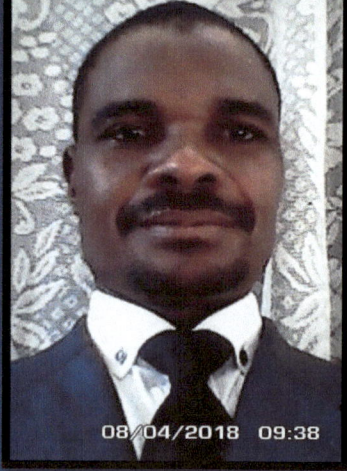

Pastor Willings Eric Chirwa
Position: Assistant Director – Malawi

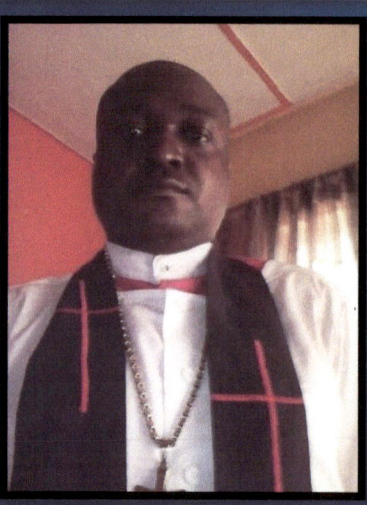

Bishop Dr. Sam Godwin
Position: Assistant Director – Nigeria

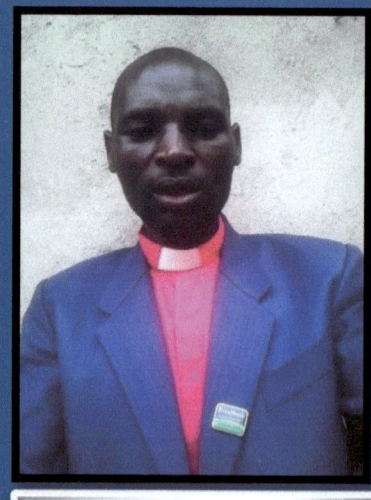

Rev. Vami Valence
Position: Assistant Director – Rwanda

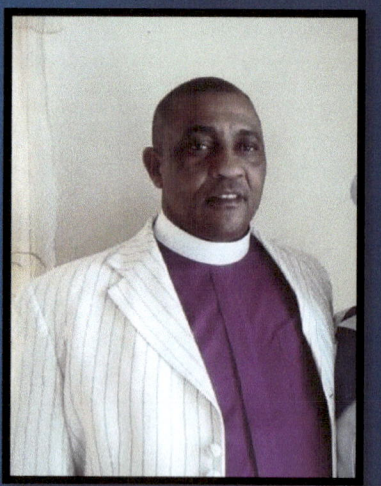

Bishop Dr. Martin Tshangela
Position: Assistant Director – South Africa

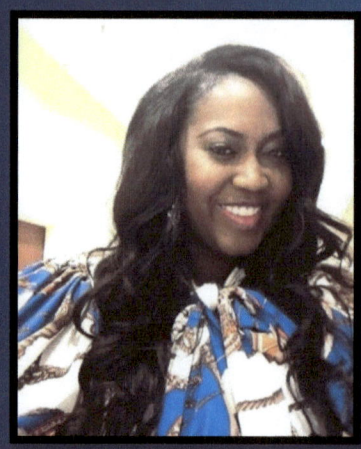

Dr. Jennifer O. Jackson
Position: Assistant Director - Texas

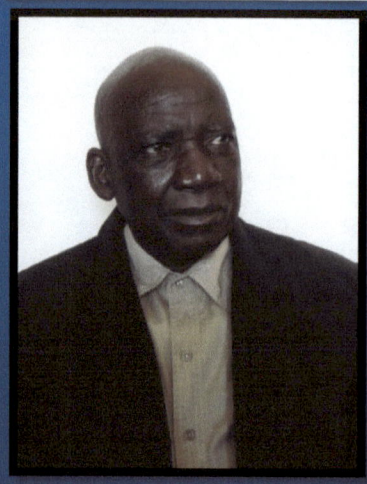

Rev. Dr. Issac Muleya
Position: Assistant Director - Zambia

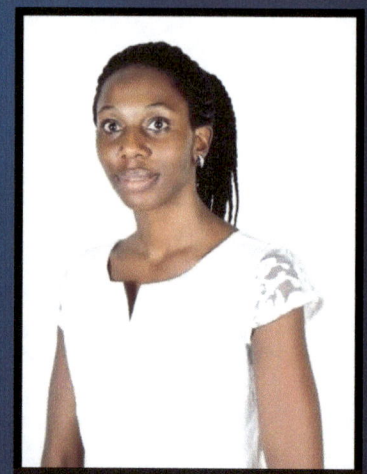

Pastor Doreen Kwesiga
Position: Assistant Director - Uganda

A few words....

Congratulations to everyone!
Happy one-year Anniversary! I am overjoyed for what the Lord is during in our Life. I call it "Promised Fulfillment." I am deeply surprised at what the Lord has done during this past year in my life and at The Grace International Bible University!

Now, many Churches and Ministers are rejoicing all around the World with a much-needed model of study and freedom that God has brought to them through GIBU. Over the year, something they did not have before, according to them, they now have. As God told me in 2009 that after 5 years of struggles, changes will occur. Is not only about my stories but the stories of the very Churches, Students, and Ministers. This makes God a God who keeps his promise. In short. GIBU has been established to work with Churches and Ministers, to bring them sound Biblical training. In this way, God had brought the World together under GIBU Leadership Biblical Supervision.

We are therefore here to offers FREE TUITION for your Bachelor's, Master's, Doctor's and PhD Degrees to students worldwide. I am inviting you to join GIBU for more knowledge in the years to Come. Happy one-year Anniversary and Congratulations!

    Rev. Dr. Rudolph Q. Kwanue, Sr. – Founder and Coordinator

As we have reached the first milestone by celebrating our First Anniversary, l believe it is OK to say that God has allowed us to prosper going from College to University in just one year. What an achievement! Following the vision of our powerful visionary Rev. Dr. Rudolph Q. Kwanue, we are educating more minority groups in free education than anyone because **EDUCATION IS OUR PASSION**! We look to the future for bigger and brighter horizons to conquer and more lives to touch and change. I pray God give us the strength to do so. To whom much is given, much is required.

    Bishop Dr. Frank A. Willet – GIBU President

Congratulations GIBU, Rev. Dr. Rudolph, Bishop Frank A. Willett, Staff, Boards, and Students for making year 1 very successful! Many students have studied hard and learned the Word of God through their Bachelor, Master, Doctor, and PhD classes! It is our hope that these students will go on to teach others what they have learned while at GIBU. In working with the GIBU as the Administrator, I have grown to know many Leaders. They all have a heart for God and only want the best for GIBU. This first year has been exciting and challenging at the same time, but God has given us Grace to see us through. Now we step into Year 2 with great anticipation as to what the new year holds for us! Keep GIBU in your prayers. This is the only University that I know of who does not charge for tuition, or make you work for it. Tuition is totally free! You can't get much better than that! This is because Rev. Dr. Rudolph has a heart for Churches and Ministers to be educated without being penniless! Again, CONGRATULATIONS GIBU!

    Faye G. Hanshew – GIBU Administrator and Graphics Designer

Congratulations and Happy Anniversary to all those involved in building GIBU in the past year. Your hard work as one team, and your experience which is internationally recognized has resulted the huge and fast growing of GIBU.

During the past year many have benefited, and the wings of GIBU continue growing as far as to the 5th Continent – Australia! Thank you for working tirelessly. You are an excellent example to many world-wide!

GIBU - Highly ranked International Online University: FREE TUITION PROGRAM! Enroll and gain the degree of your choice.

Bishop Dr. Yebiyo Ghebrezghi – Board of Trustees and Director of DRC

Congratulations to the Grace International Bible University for one year of operating success. Operating a University is hard work which requires strong leaders with a strong vision. As G.I.B.U. enters now its second year, leaders such as Founder and Director, Dr. Rudolph Kwanue, President, Bishop Frank Willett, Vice President, Dr. Jimmie Vaughn, Administrator, Dr. Faye G. Hanshew, all directors, trustees and staff must continue to put your faith in the guidance of the Holy Spirit for direction, insight, and the revelation required to lead nations of students into a proper education, enabling them to teach, instruct, and preach the Word of God. I thank God for anyone who possess the humility, yet the vision to take on the world in like manner when Father God sent Jesus to give Himself for the benefit of the whole world.

Congratulations,

Bishop, Dr. Bill Hanshew
World Bible School International Training Center, Joplin, Missouri, USA
G.I.B.U. International Consultant
I.A.C.E. International Director

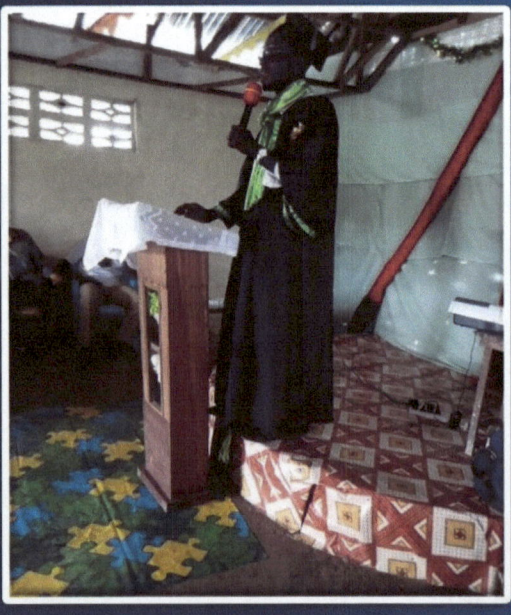
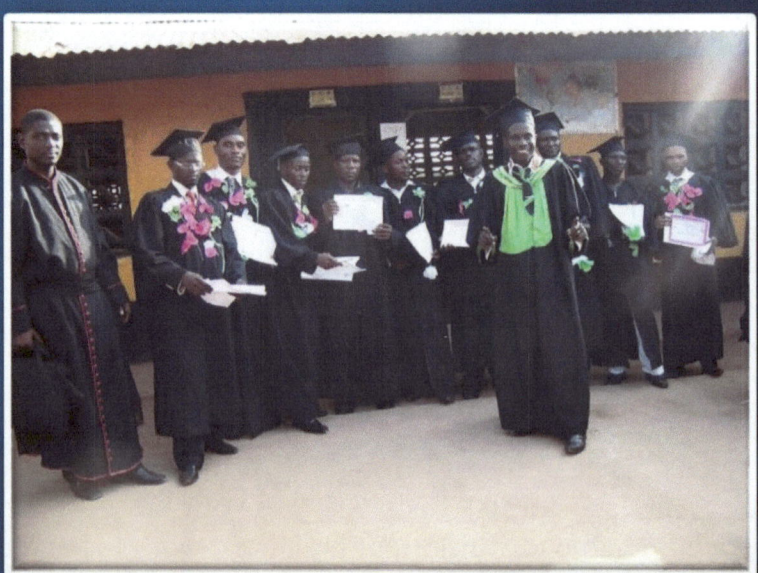

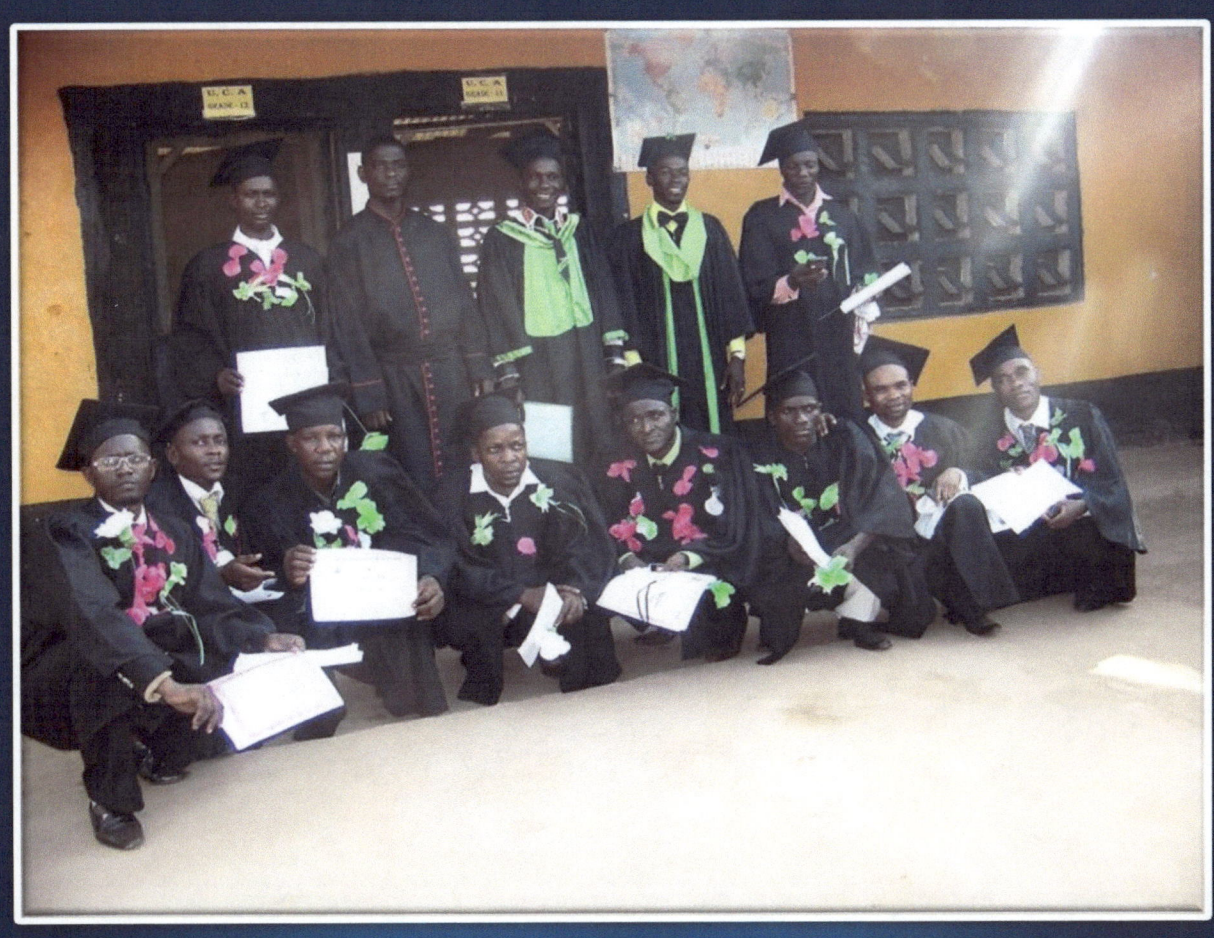
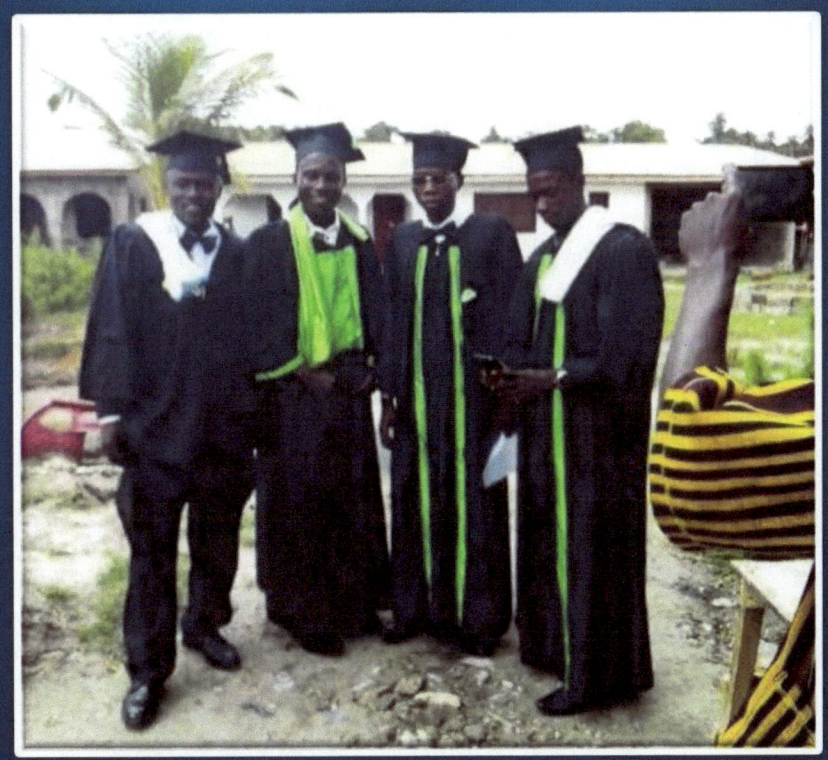

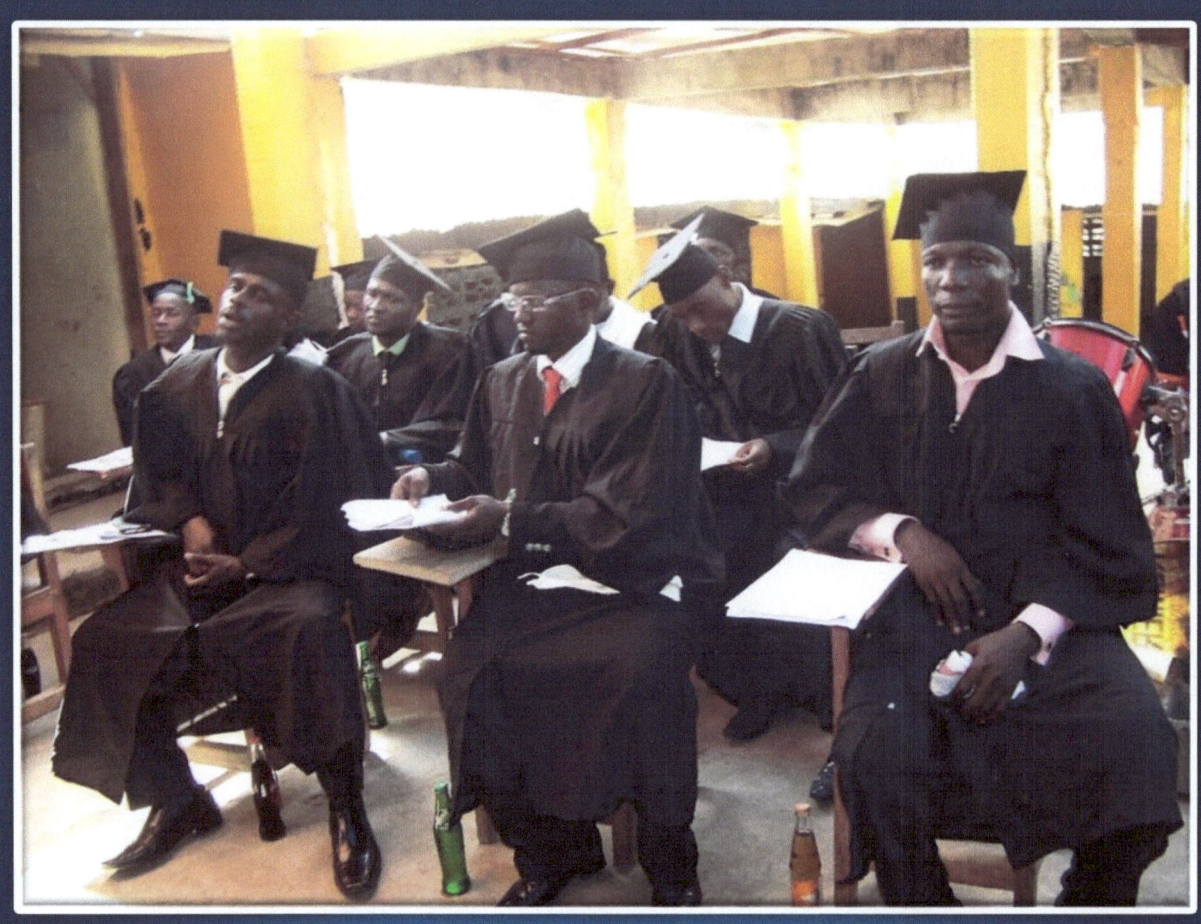
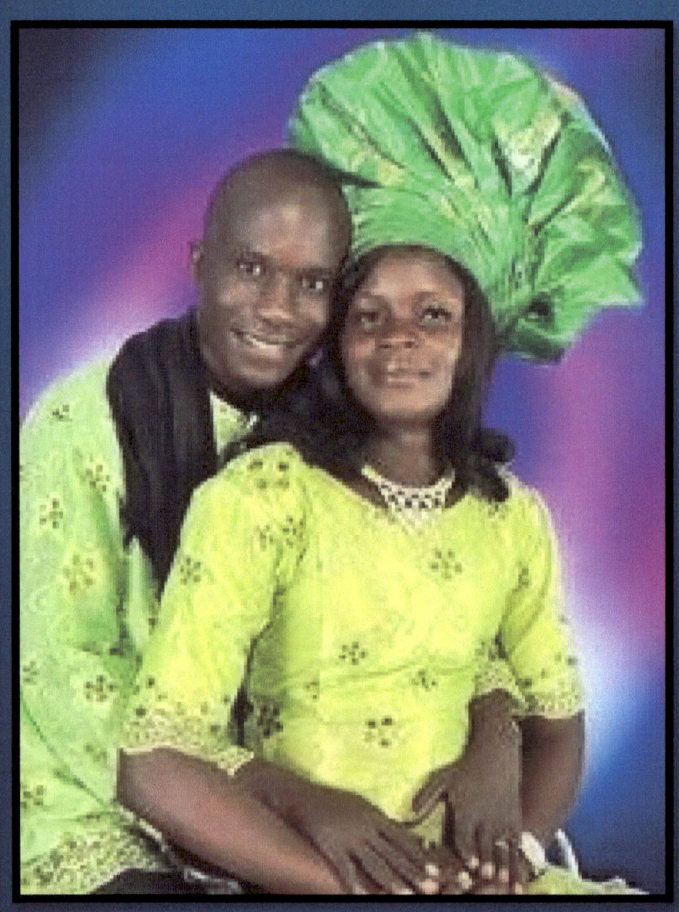

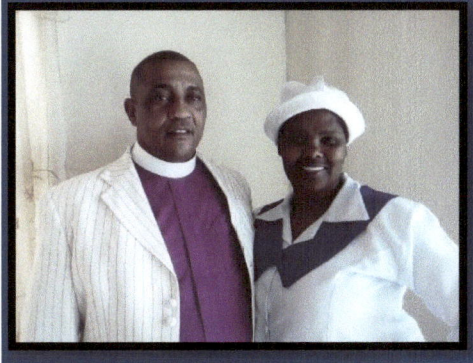
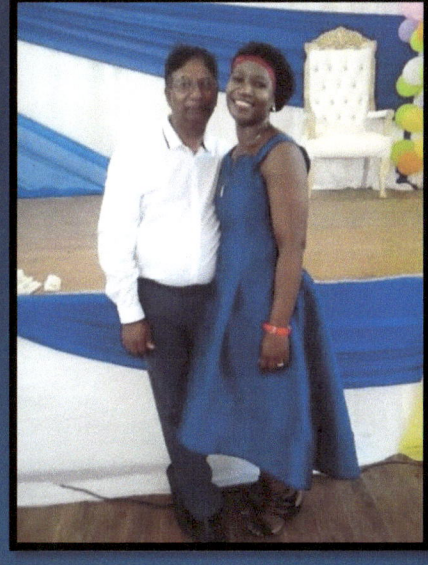
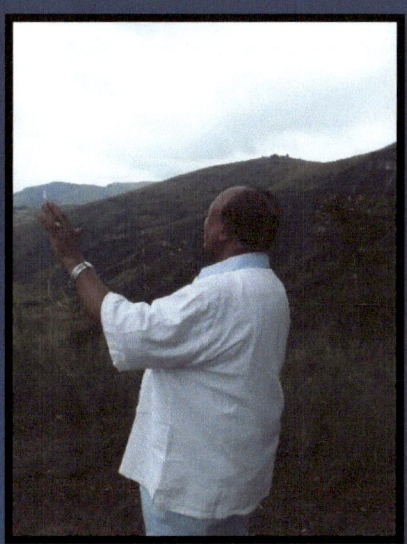
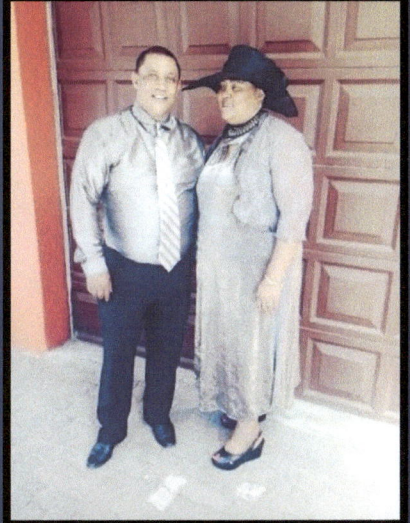
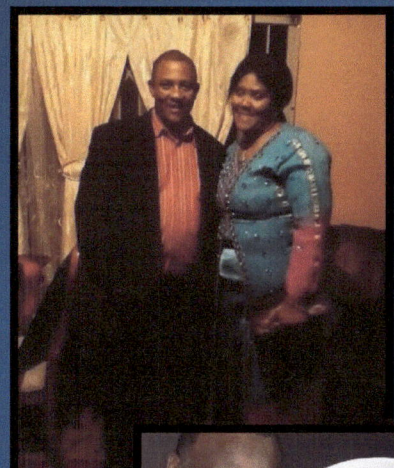
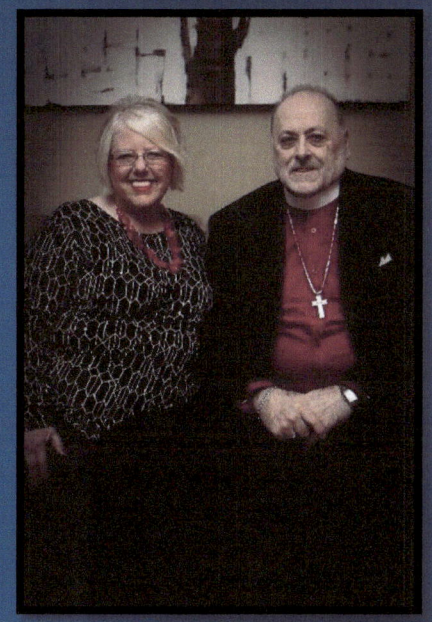
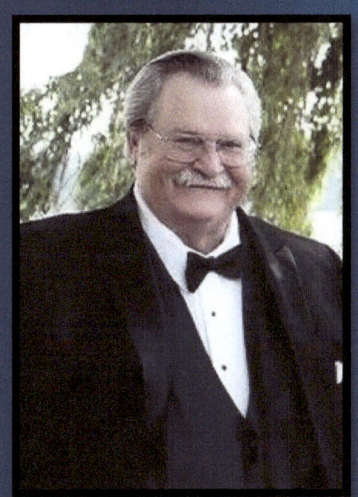
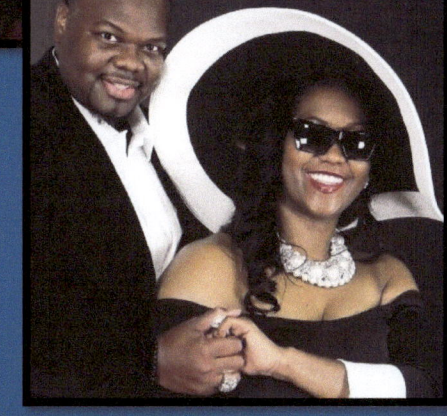
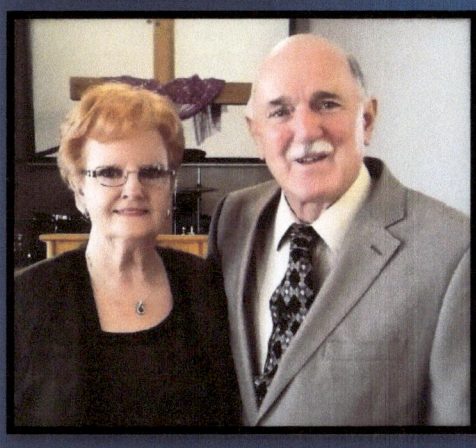
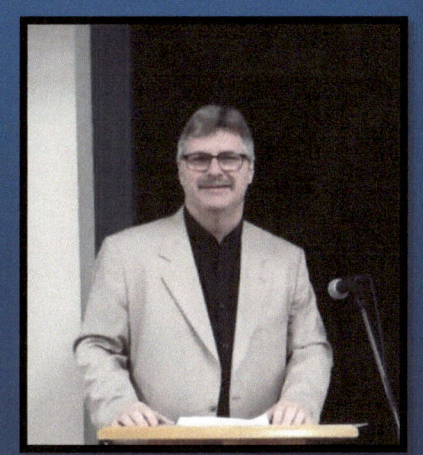
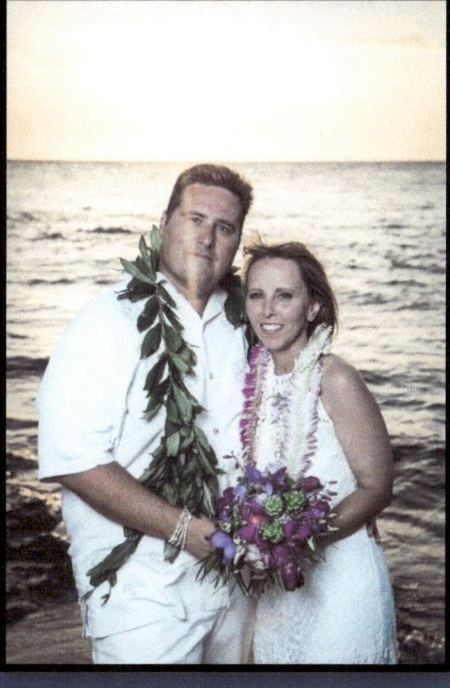

Grace International Bible University

IS ACCREDITED BY:
THE WORLD-WIDE ACCREDITATION COMMISSION OF CHRISTIAN EDUCATION INSTITUTIONS

The Full Gospel of Christ Fellowship, Inc.
Drs. Paul & Faye Richardson
2800 Blendwell Rd.
Richmond, Va. 23224
804-276-4709

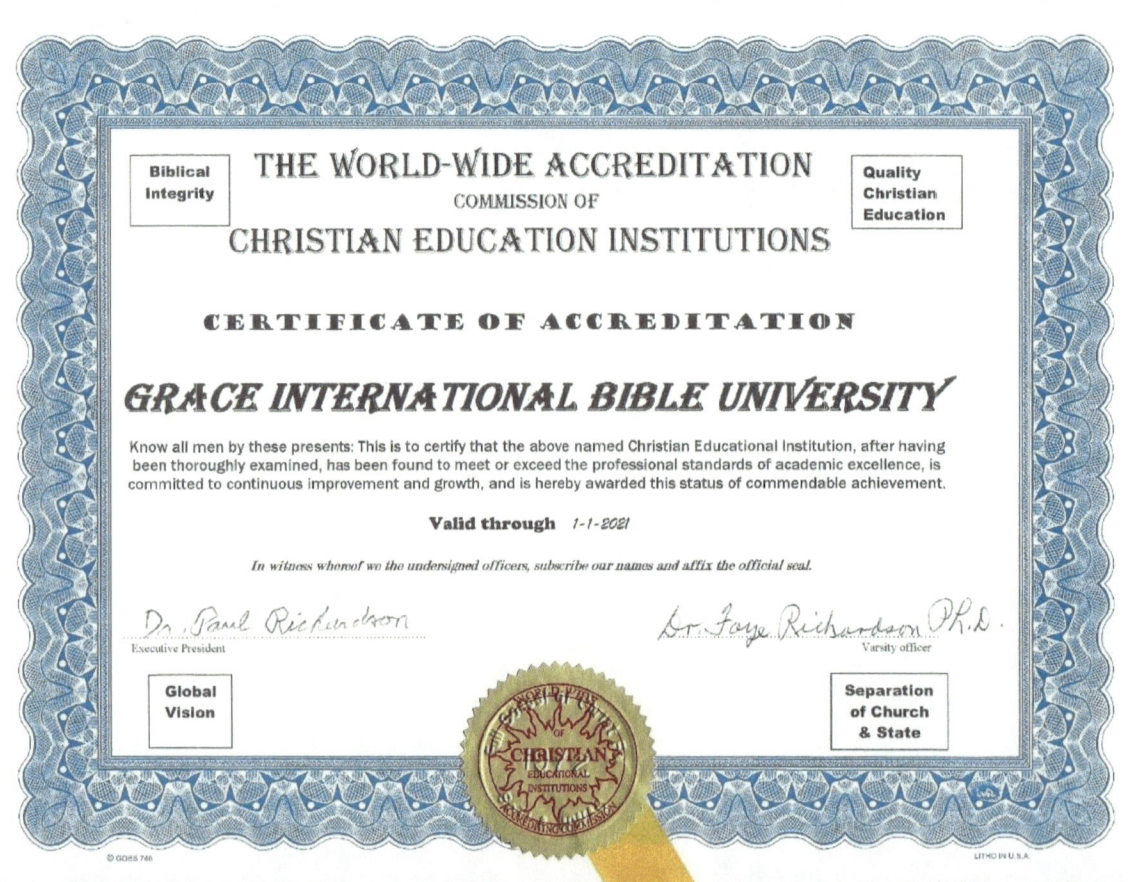

THE WORLD-WIDE ACCREDITATION COMMISSION OF CHRISTIAN EDUCATION INSTITUTIONS

Biblical Integrity | Quality Christian Education

CERTIFICATE OF ACCREDITATION

GRACE INTERNATIONAL BIBLE UNIVERSITY

Know all men by these presents: This is to certify that the above named Christian Educational Institution, after having been thoroughly examined, has been found to meet or exceed the professional standards of academic excellence, is committed to continuous improvement and growth, and is hereby awarded this status of commendable achievement.

Valid through 1-1-2021

In witness whereof we the undersigned officers, subscribe our names and affix the official seal.

Dr. Paul Richardson — Executive President
Dr. Faye Richardson Ph.D. — Varsity officer

Global Vision | Separation of Church & State

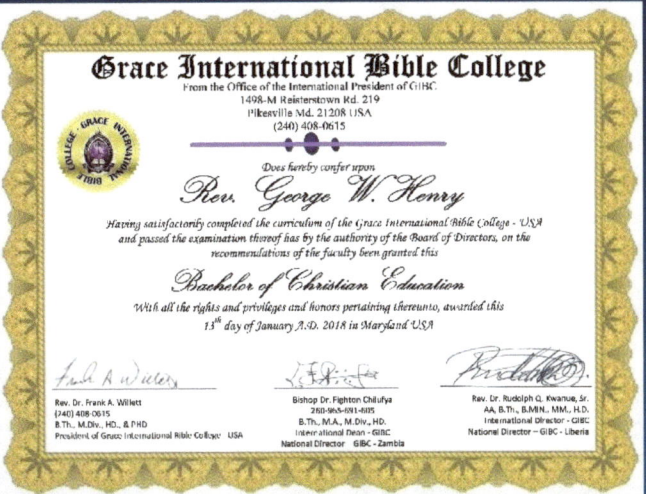
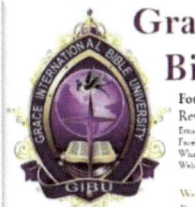
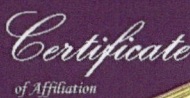

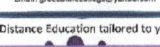
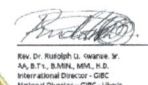

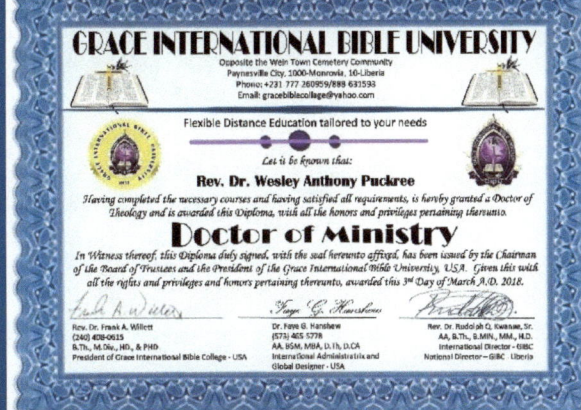
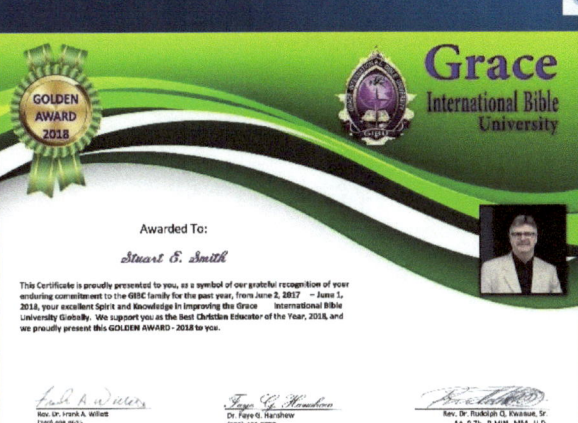

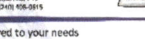
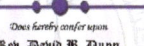
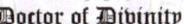
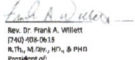
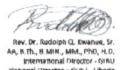

And during GIBU's First Year, We Welcomed IACE International Accreditation Commission for Education!

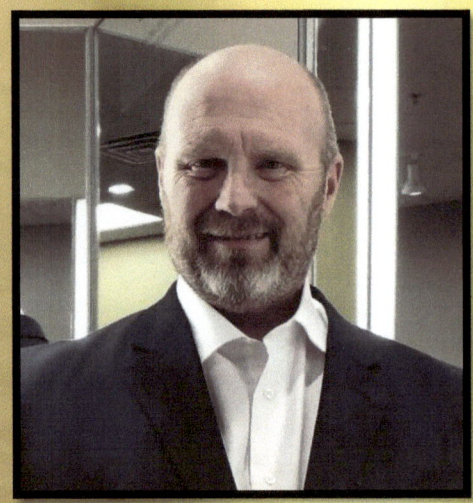

Bishop Benjamin Paris
President - IACE

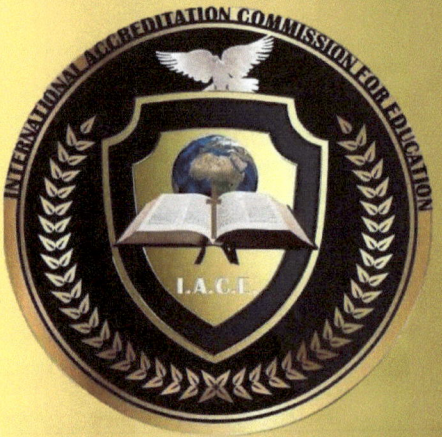

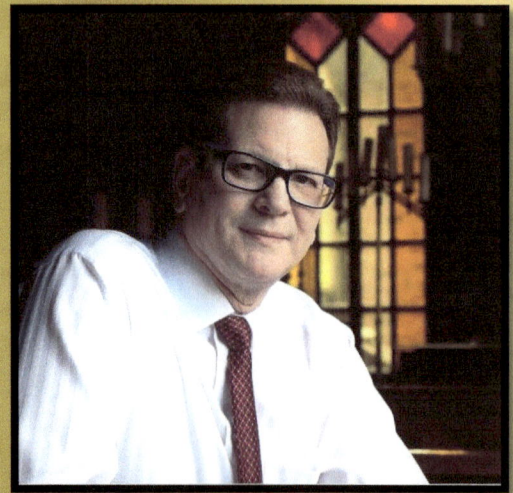

Dr. Charles Sathmary
Vice-President - IACE

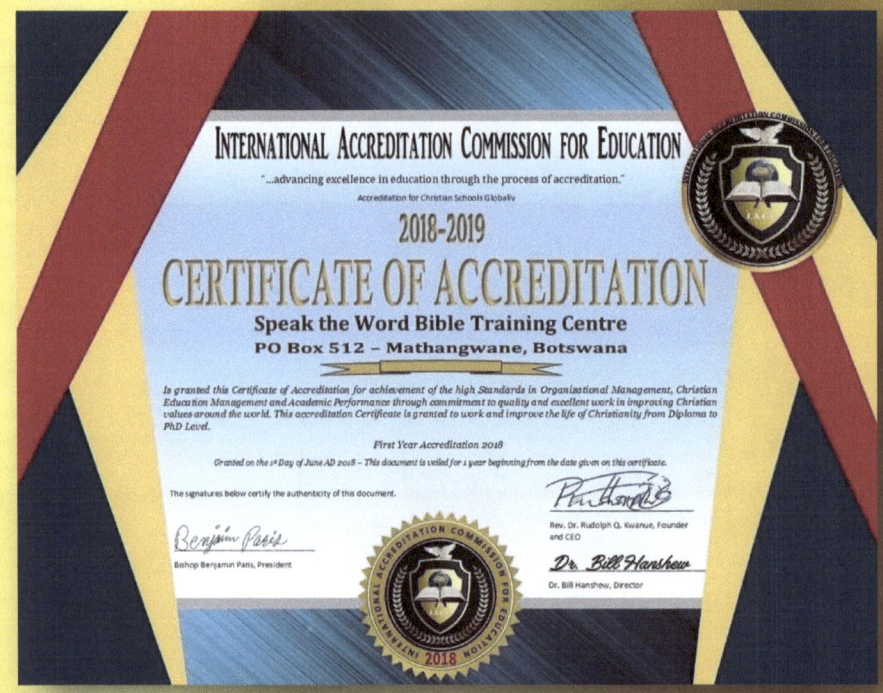

God's Lawnmower

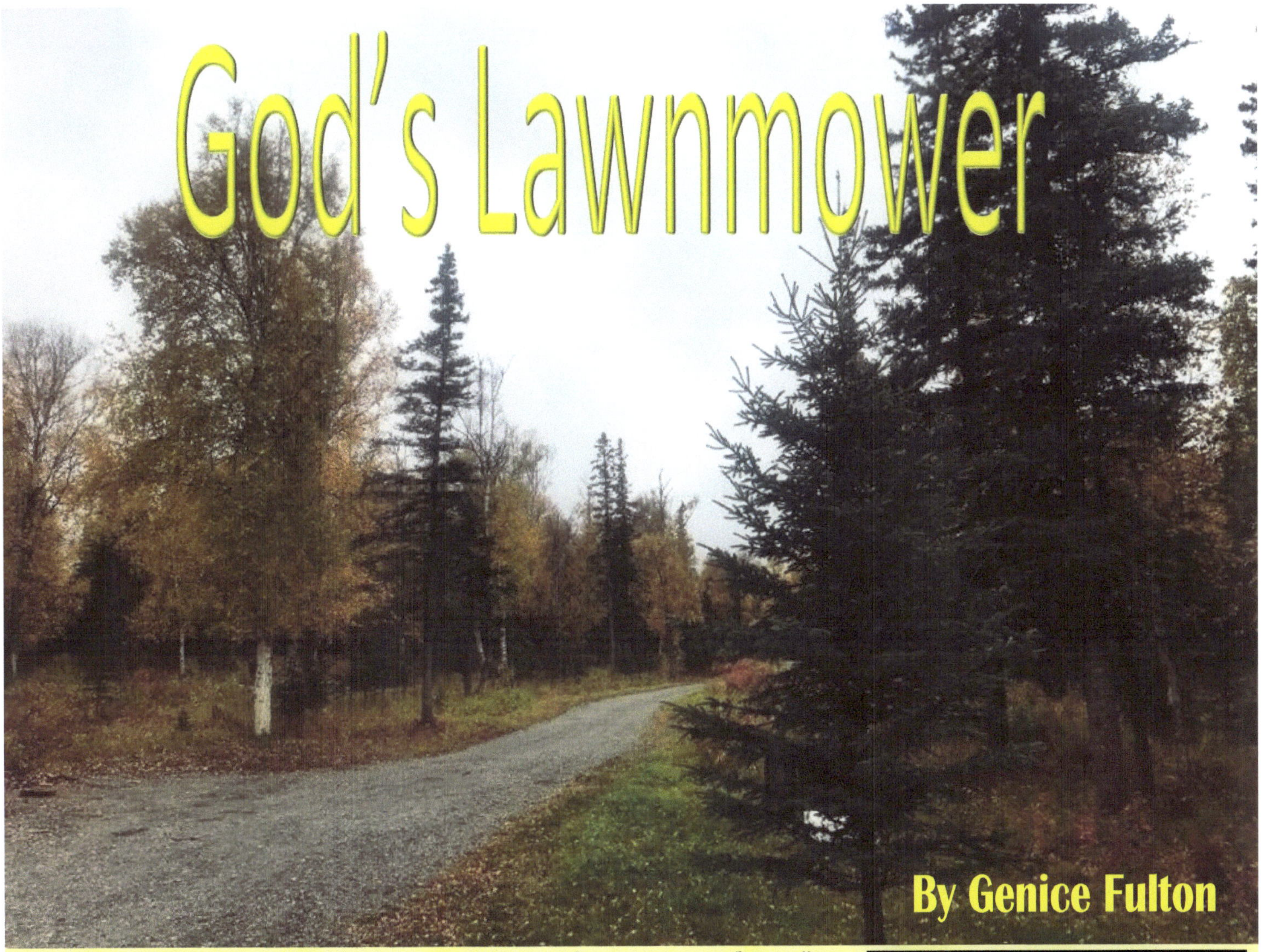

By Genice Fulton

I was recently in a series of church services with Evangelist Ivan Tait with What Matters Ministry (http://whatmattersmm.org).

In one service, he explained true repentance as something like this. If you borrow someone's lawnmower and you break it (purposely or accidentally) you don't return the lawnmower broken. You don't hide or ignore the fact you broke the lawnmower hoping no one sees or brings it to your attention. You own up, walk in integrity, and go buy that person a new lawnmower that is better than the one you borrowed. You take the lawnmower to the person and say, "I broke your lawnmower. I'm so sorry. Here is a new one, a better one to replace the one I broke. Please forgive me." That is true repentance.

Some readers may be thinking, "Wow, that is expensive." Yes, it is because sin (hurting others) is costly for all involved. (Romans 6:23)

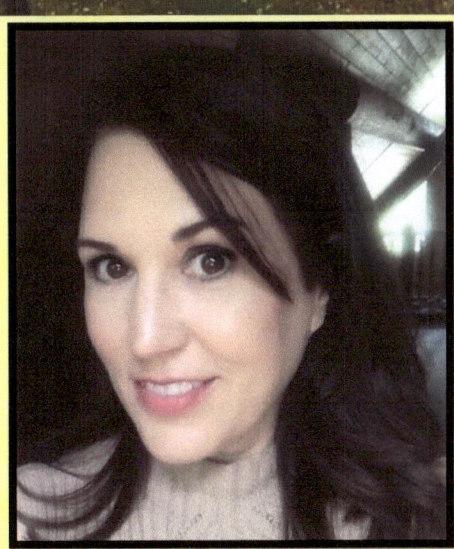

I went home that night and I had a dream. I dreamed I was upset over my broken lawnmower. In the dream I was sitting in my yard on my knees looking at my broken lawnmower. It was a beautiful day, a really nice spring morning. The sun was shining, and the grass was really green. There was a cool spring breeze. I was sitting on the ground by my old, broken down, oily, dirty lawnmower covered in old brown dead grass. I had my face in my hands crying. The

LORD had compassion on me. He walked up to me, placed His hand on my shoulder and asked me what was wrong. I said, "He won't ever give me that new lawnmower." He responded, "That's ok Baby. I will give you a new lawnmower and My lawnmowers are the best! You can't get any better than My lawnmowers!"

REJOICE!! Rejoice in Him always!! And again, I say REJOICE!! He has given me my new lawnmower!!

I rarely am given the interpretation of my own dreams, but God gave me the interpretation of this dream.

• I was wounded from a person who has never truly repented restoring the relationship. He had placed the burden of forgiveness on me while ignoring the damage that had been done.

• I was upset the person hadn't repented, made things right, and worked toward real restoration. Instead he ignored the impact of repeated derogatory actions. While continuing to expect me to fully trust and act as if nothing ever happened. (Did I mention, repeatedly?) Expecting more of me than he would ever give if the tables were turned. But joy always comes in the morning! God promised it and He always sees to it! (Psalm 30:5)

• I was so hurt and teetering on the edge of hopelessness. I was praying and walking in faith. I was trusting in what God was doing on my behalf and having faith in Him and His Word. He works all things together for my good! He always causes me to triumph! (Romans 8:28, 2 Corinthians 2:14, Psalm 9:10)

• God didn't have to ask what was wrong. He "knows all about me." He wants to hear from us. He wants to be involved and included in every aspect of our lives! The good, the bad, and the ugly because He is a true friend! He has numbered every hair on my head! He watches over me! (Jeremiah 33:3, Psalm 139: 1- 24, Psalm 145:9, John 15:15, Matthew 10:30, Psalm 121:5)

• Over the course of the last four years, when all I wanted to do was give up, walk away and disappear. When I had regained hope but then lost all hope, repeatedly. When I had to fight myself (which was the worst) not to abandon the relationship after being disappointed and hurt over and over and over again. When I began to wonder, and it appeared everyone around me was encouraged and significant (even the one who hurt me) except me. About the time I was completely hopeless I refused to give up and I continued to put one foot in front of the other (and crawled on the days when I couldn't walk). I kept doing what I didn't feel like doing, and I kept my eyes on what God wanted me to do in the situation. I kept my eyes on God instead of the situation. I set myself aside and focused on God and made God's kingdom and what His Word says the priority over the hurt and the unknown future. I definitely didn't walk in perfection and I stumbled many times. Now, in all His goodness and faithfulness and in due season God is giving me my "new lawnmower!" God is giving me a brand-new start! A start without the hurt. He has supernaturally healed the broken places! Where I was dead, He had made me alive again! He has chased me down, made all things new, and now I can continue to press on! Hallelujah!!! (1 Corinthians 1:9, Psalm 136:1, Galatians 6:9, Isaiah 61:3, Psalm 23:6, Philippians 3:14)

Please make time to read the 23rd chapter of Joshua. I personally know verse three of the twenty-third chapter of Joshua to be completely true. I "have seen everything the LORD my God has done for me during my lifetime. The LORD has fought for me against my enemies."

Please pay special attention to what I believe God has shown me in verses seven through eleven in the twenty-third chapter of Joshua. I am to "make sure I do not associate with other people still remaining in the land. I won't even mention the names of their gods, much less swear by them or serve them or worship them." The enemies in my life have been lack, poverty, abuse, neglect, and lies. I will "cling tightly to the LORD my God as I have done!

For "the LORD has driven out all" things not of Him and "they have not been able to defeat me!" I "put a thousand to flight, for my God fights for me just as He promised!" To keep this fight in forward momentum in my favor, I "love the LORD my God by keeping His commands."

Deep in my heart I know that every promise of the LORD my God has come true! Not a single one has failed! (Joshua 23:14)

When you discover someone has "broken your lawnmower, covered the matter up, refuses to acknowledge they broke it, and refuses to replace it" (genuine repentance) … do not despair, rejoice! God has everything you need! Cling to Him through every breath! (Psalm 50:10-12)

Even though the person refuses to make it right…God is making it right and there is no right right-er than God's! (Isaiah 43:19)

Over the past four years during this hardship, God has repeatedly told me:

- Matt 6:33
- Philippians 4:8
- Psalm 9:10
- Proverbs 4:23
- Galatians 6:9

If you are in a seemingly hopeless situation, cling to Him and His Word. Never give up on God's Word! He is watching, and He is fighting for you! (Jeremiah 1:12, 1 John 5:14 & 15)

(Philippians 4:4, Isaiah 61:3, Psalm 30:11-12, Psalm 30:5, Romans 8:28, 2 Corinthians 2:14, Psalm 9:10, Jeremiah 33:3, Psalm 139: 1- 24, Psalm 145:9, John 15:15, Matthew 10:30, Psalm 121:5 1 Corinthians 1:9, Psalm 136:1, Galatians 6:9, Isaiah 61:3, Matthew 6:33, Philippians 4:8, Psalm 9:10, Proverbs 4:23, Galatians 6:9)

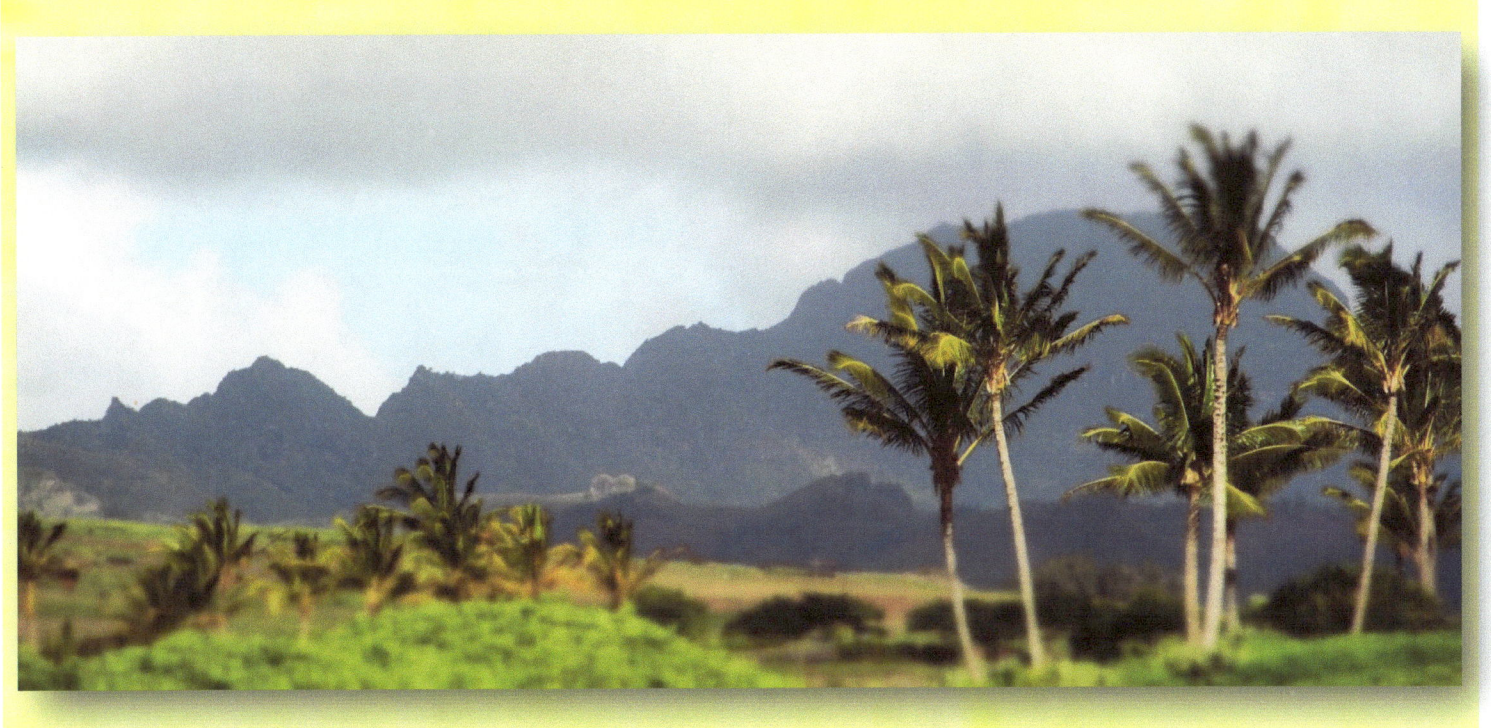

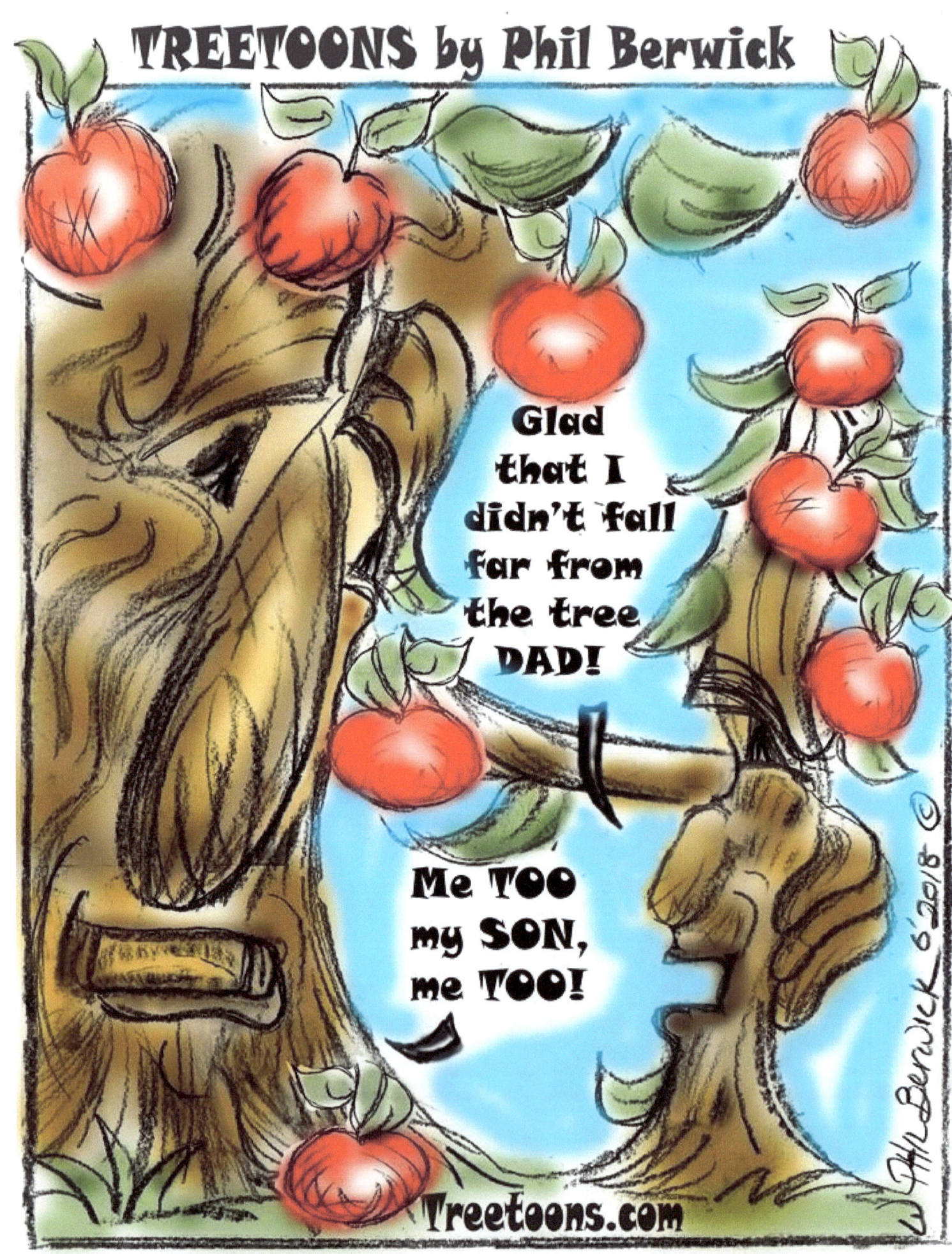

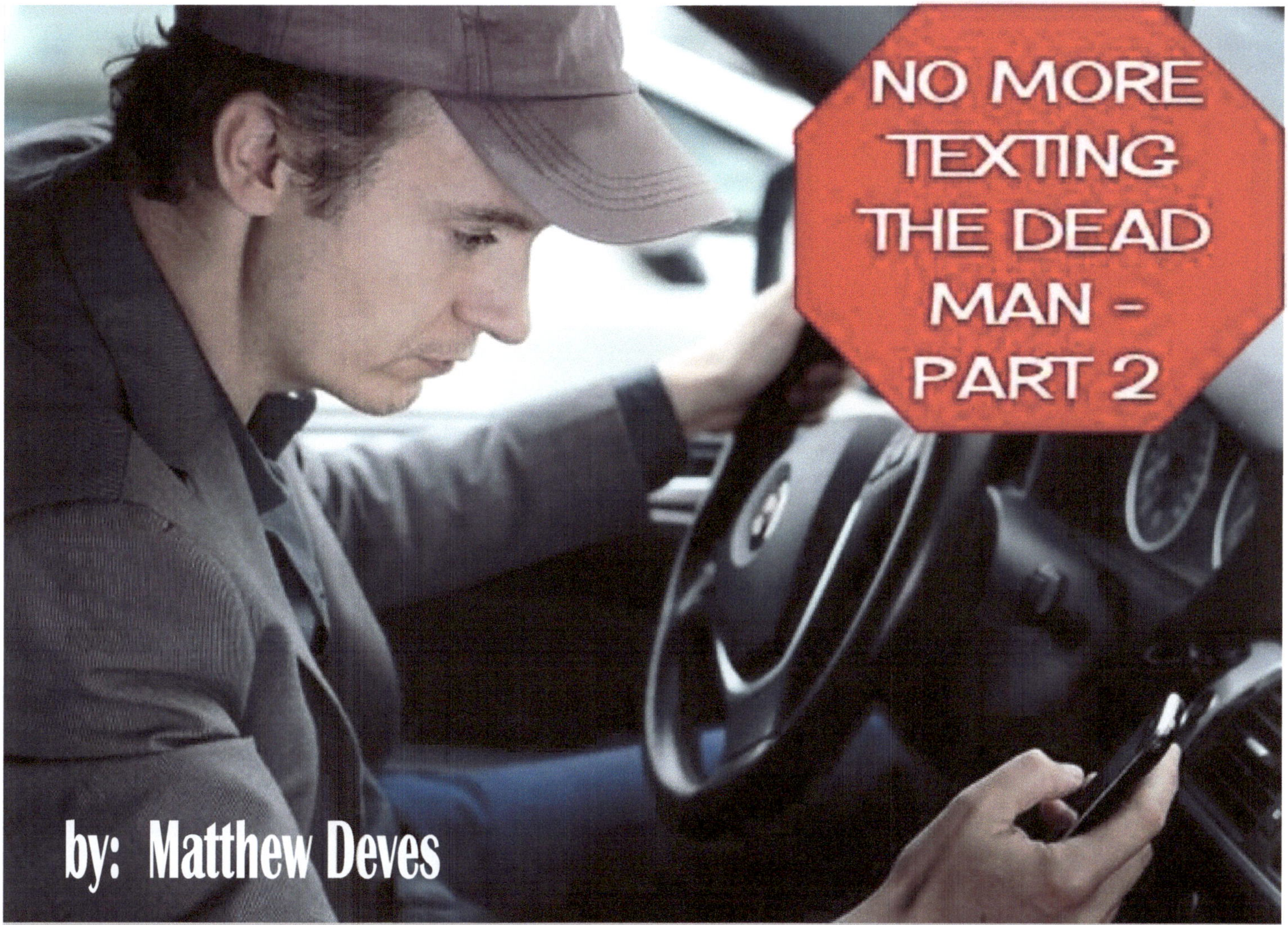

NO MORE TEXTING THE DEAD MAN – PART 2

by: Matthew Deves

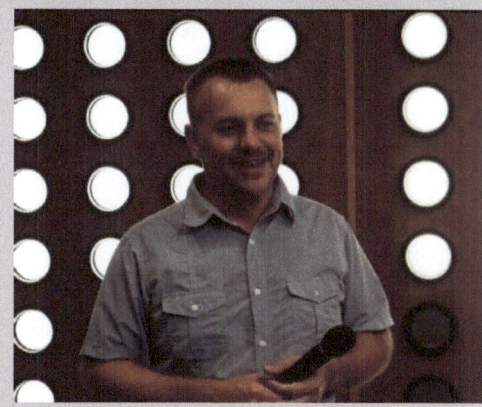

God doesn't speak to the old-man. Neither should you. That guy is dead. There is a reason why God says not to communicate with the dead. (Deuteronomy 18:11) They only give advice that is lifeless. That old nature should not be consulted. It will ask you to analyze your past failures. What could have been. What you should have done. This causes mental pain and suffering. This can replay over and over in your head causing it to ache. The mental hamster-wheel can be exhausting. Eventually, your brain needs a rest and will take one even when you resist. Why not stop the hurting now? You may feel like you can't stop the madness but ask yourself, "Are we under any obligation to the dead man? Do I owe it answers?"

So, don't you see that we don't owe this old do-it-yourself life one red cent. There's nothing in it for us, nothing at all. The best thing to do is give it a decent burial and get on with your new life. God's Spirit beckons. There are things to do and places to go! This resurrection life you received from God is not a timid, grave-tending life. It's adventurously expectant, greeting God with a childlike "What's next, Papa?" Romans 8:12-15 Message Bible

A decent burial ceremony was finished when you were baptized. That old-self was "...buried therefore with Him by the baptism into death, so that just as Christ was raised from the dead by the glorious [power] of the Father, so we too might [habitually] live and behave in newness of life." Romans 6:4 AMP

Your job description as a believer does not include the words, "grave-tender!"

Stop texting your old-nature. It's dead. Put it off permanently. Block the number. "Lie not one to another, having put off the old man with his practices." Colossians 3:9 (YLT) Start by not lying to yourself. The old-man has nothing for you.

Therefore, if any person is [ingrafted] in Christ (the Messiah) he is a new creation (a new creature altogether); the old [previous moral and spiritual condition] has passed away. Behold, the fresh and new has come! 2 Corinthians 5:17 AMP.

Your fresh and new life has arrived! The old nature is where the pain ruled. We had no way out. Jesus took the pain and gave you an escape. Leave the pain

The promise is given in Isaiah...
Isaiah 53:4 Surely He has borne our griefs (sicknesses, weaknesses, and distresses) and carried our sorrows and pains [of punishment], yet we [ignorantly] considered Him stricken, smitten, and afflicted by God [as if with leprosy]. [Matthew 8:17.]

The promise fulfilled in Matthew...
Matthew 8:17 And thus He fulfilled what was spoken by the prophet Isaiah, He Himself took [in order to carry away] our weaknesses and infirmities and bore away our diseases. [Isaiah 53:4.]

The Thayer Definition of "infirmities" or asthenia in this verse can mean, "want of strength or weakness...of the soul."
Weakness of the mind, will, and emotions. That's mental stress. Jesus took the headache caused by the mental stress by giving you His Life.

That ye put away, as concerning your former manner of life, the old man, that waxeth corrupt after the lusts of deceit Ephesians 4:22 KJV

That you have put off once for all with reference to your former manner of life the old man which is being corrupted according to the passionate desires of deceit; moreover, that you are being constantly renewed with reference to the spirit of your mind; and that you have put on once for all the new man which after God was created in righteousness and holiness of truth. Ephesians 4:22-24 Wuest translation

Of verse 24, the Wuest Word studies give us some incredible insight, "The third fact in the teaching is that they "put on the new man." The word "new" is kainos, not new in point of time, which would be neos, but new in point of quality, new in quality as opposed to the old in the sense of outworn, marred through age, which latter designations refer to the old man. "Man" is again anthrōpos, the individual. Since the old man refers to the unsaved person dominated by the totally depraved nature, the new man refers to the saved person dominated by the divine nature. This new man "after God is created in righteousness and true holiness." This is what Paul has reference to when he says, "Therefore if any man be in Christ, he is a new creation" (2Corinthians 5:17). "After God" is kata theon, "according to what God is in Himself," that is, created after the pattern of what God is. The expression "true holiness" could better be rendered, "holiness of truth," "truth" being personified and being opposed to the "deceit" of verse 22 which was also personified.

Put on the "new man." God speaks to you through your new nature. He communicates to you in true righteousness and holiness.

Now if all were included in his death they were equally included in his resurrection. This unveiling of his love redefines human life! Whatever reference we could have of ourselves outside of our association with Christ is no longer relevant. 2 Corinthians 5:15 Mirror Bible.

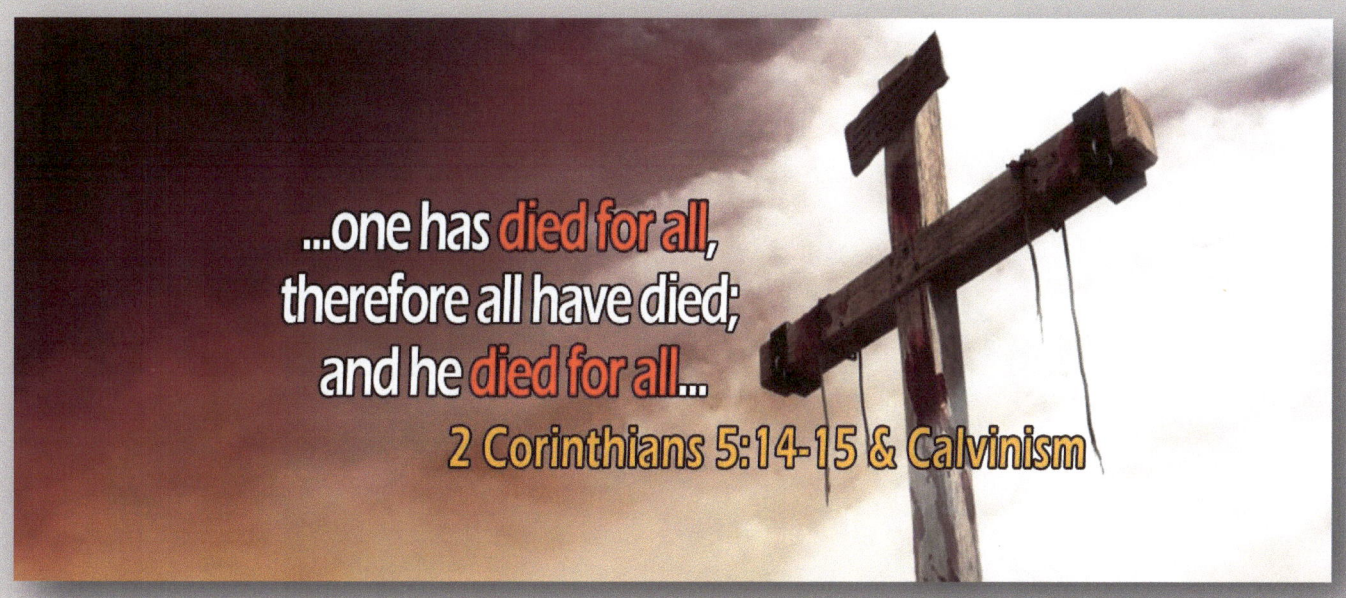

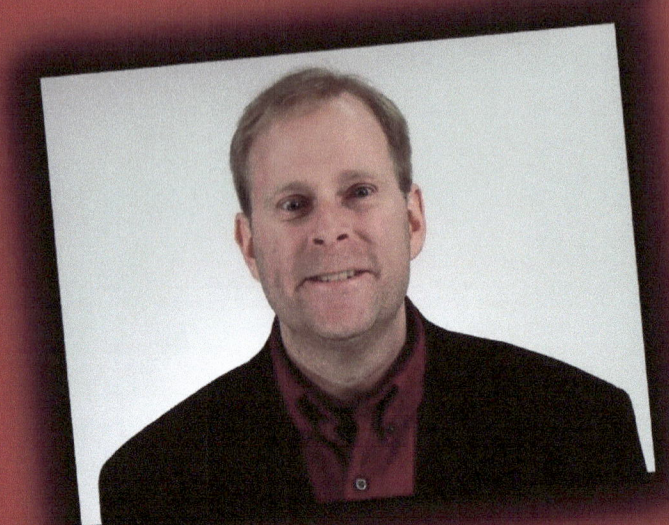

DO WE FEAR DEATH – OF THE OLD MAN?

by: Dr. Richard W. Rundell

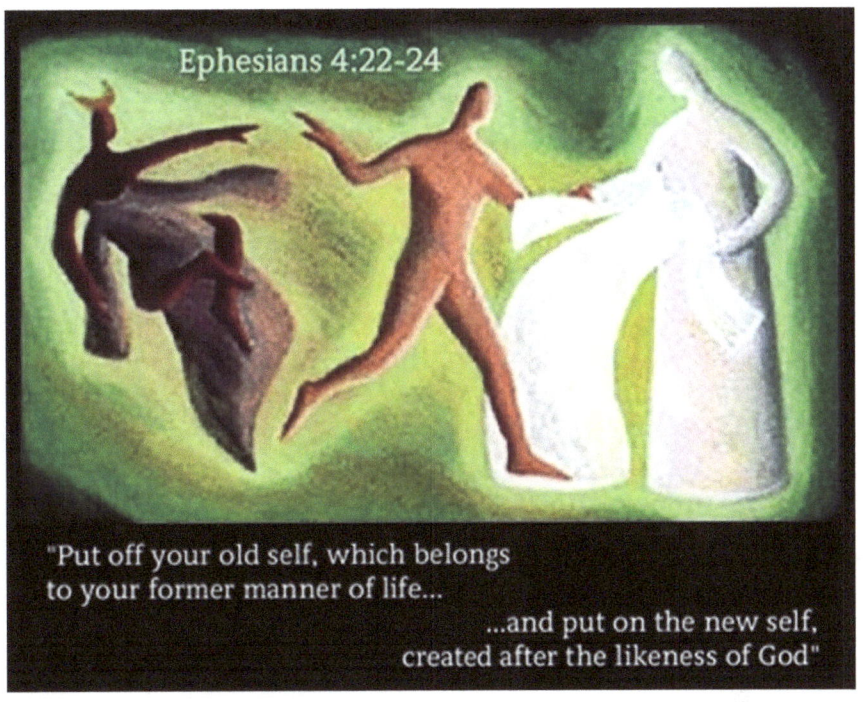

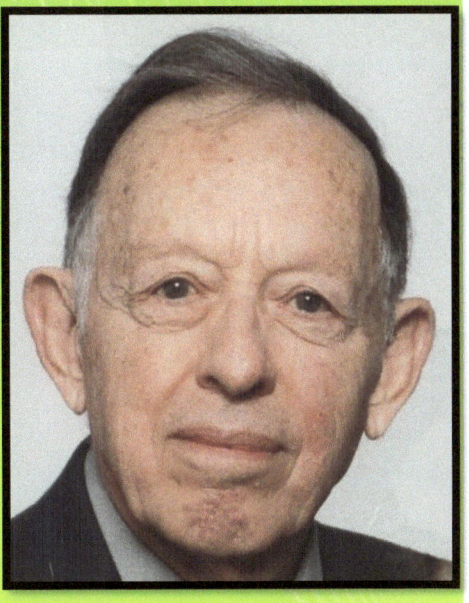

Let us consider Ephesians 4:22-24 NKJV, "that you put off, concerning your former conduct, the old man which grows corrupt according to the deceitful lusts, and be renewed in the spirit of your mind, and that you put on the new man which was created according to God, in true righteousness and holiness."

Paul compared our Christian life to stripping off our dirty clothes of a sinful past and putting on the snowy white robes of Christ's righteousness.

The bible declares our old man is dead, yet we have memories of the past that we like to rehearse in our mind, memories of our old nature, even negative thoughts of our old life.

If we turn our life over to the Lord, do we fear losing the keys to our identity? Those little subtle personality quirks we have enjoyed in the past? Turning our life over to the Lord amounts to a transition from a life we know to a life of the unknown. What will my life as a Christian be like? Will I have to give up all I've known?

If our old man is really dead, dead to our former identity, dead to the cares and mistakes of the past, then do we fear losing our identity? We should feel no pain or regret; we have turned all our cares to the Lord.

When we first hear the question, "Do you fear death," we immediately think of our body dying, going to the grave, giving up all we experienced as our life of 40, 50 or more years. But rather let us consider the death of our old man, that is, do we have a fear of giving up all our former ways of life, under our Adamic nature. We have settled in our comfort zone or should we say zones, those choice practices or pet habits that have become an integral part of us, even those we know we should scrap.

Just days before my salvation experience at the Lay Witness Mission program at our local church, I sensed the Lord leading me to accept Him as my Savior, and yet I wondered, "Would I have to give up my favorite TV shows, and ball games, would I have to spend all my time in church? I didn't realize that it was some of my "personality" the Lord wanted me to give up, mainly my self-righteousness but also my critical, judgmental spirit.

Many people fear that if they turn their life over to the Lord, they will have to give up their right to control their own life. They reason that they know what they want to do, and they don't want God to interfere.

The fear of the death of our Adamic nature is so subtle, and mostly in our subconscious mind. We cling to the memories of our childhood and seek to anchor our identity in those memories. "and release those who through fear of death were their entire lifetime subject to bondage" (Heb. 2:15. NKJV).

What is sown is not made alive unless it dies (1 Cor. 15:36). Death then is a necessary perquisite in order to bring forth new forms of life. Death (of our self-will, our old man) frees us from sin (Rom. 6:7). Death is swallowed up in victory. (1 Cor. 15:54). What a blessed promise.

Paul presents the results of Christ's death for the believer and the believer's death with Him. Because believers are united with Jesus both in His death and resurrection, they participate in the new creation. "Therefore, if anyone is in Christ, he is a new creation; old things have passed away; behold, all things have become new" (2 Cor. 5:17). A born-again Christian should welcome the death of the old man.

Fear of natural death implies fear of the unknown, "What will heaven or the other side of the grave be like? Am I convinced of eternal life?" We've spent so many years in our comfort zone. But what about fear of losing our identity? We are not talking about our identity as an office or factory worker, school teacher or store clerk. Rather we speak of our philosophy of life, how we relate to God and our role in society as a Christian. What about the people with whom we socialize, what was our role or reputation in the community, a leader or follower?

Unfortunately, today politics has enforced on the public fear of offending someone. That speaks of another fear and another lesson. But God has not given us a spirit of fear (2 Tim. 1:7).

We try to hang on to that independent spirit, that stubborn spirit, selfish spirit; we feel that's who we are, wanting to do things our way.

Do we really believe our old man is dead? How come we try to resurrect him? If we turn our life over to the Lord, do we fear losing part of our personality, our identity?

By fully accepting Christ's work on the cross, we can live free of any and all fear. We must discern those characteristics of our personality that are displeasing to God and begin to deal with them. Even after conversion, we may cling to a few random remnants of the old man.

The nature of man seems to draw him to become a slave to something. Either some habit, the computer, social media, or electronic devices, smoking, hobby, TV, or anything of the world. Paul said he become a love slave to Christ. We have to live as a new Christian.

We don't want to give up who we are or who we think we are, that is, our basic personality, our former identity. It's more important that we get rid of our self-righteous, critical, judgmental spirit as well as the negative memories of our past. If we turn our life over to the Lord, do we fear losing the keys to our identity? Those little subtle personality quirks we have enjoyed in the past?

Turning our life over to the Lord amounts to a transition from a life we know to a life of the unknown. What will my life as a Christian be like? Will I have to give up all I've known? We choose to believe, and we choose to follow the Lord rather than our flesh.

UNDERSTANDING SALVATIONAL VOCABULARY – Part 2

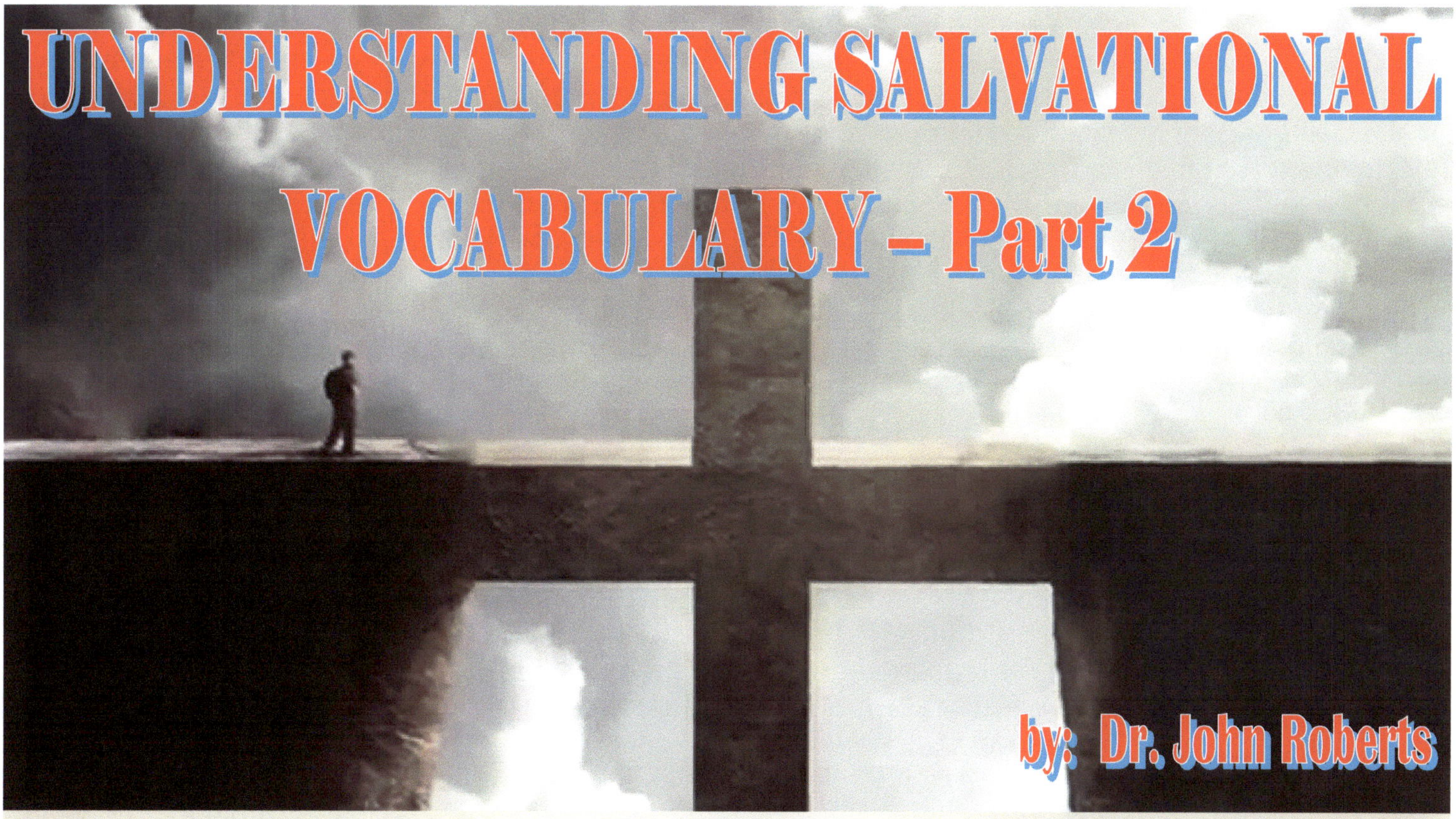

by: Dr. John Roberts

4. Propitiation: (1 John 2:2) "And He (Christ) is the propitiation for our sins: and not for ours only, but also for the sins of the whole world." Propitiation's method is understood in two passages (Rom.3:25). "Being justified freely by His grace through the redemption that is IN CHRIST Jesus: Whom God hath set forth to be a propitiation thru faith in His Blood." Ephesians 2:13 declares, "But now in Christ Jesus ye who sometimes were far off are made nigh by the Blood of Christ." Propitiation is not only central to Salvation but is necessary. Why? Because of God's wrath which obviously stemmed from a very stern reaction of the Divine nature to the very nature of sinful man. In the Old Testament propitiation held a temporary place, and that as at the Mercy Seat found in the Tabernacle of Moses. In the New Testament propitiation had a permanent place, and that is the center cross in Golgotha. The permanent results of propitiation meant that God is justified in forgiving sin. It also meant that God is justified in bestowing righteousness.

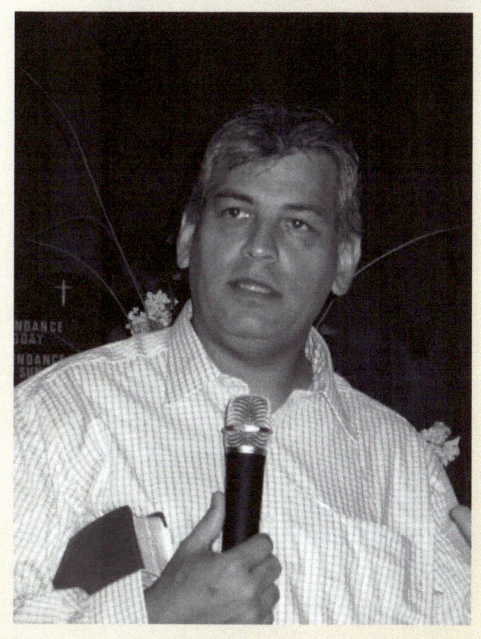

5. Remission: "To Him (Jesus) gave all the prophets witness, that thru His name whosoever believeth in Him shall receive remission of sins." Remission means RE+MISSION. In other words, the term is synonymous with the word forgiveness. It refers to a sending back, or a putting away. The original word is discovered in Matthew 1:19; and Hebrews 9:26. However, in Luke 6:37; Ephesians 4:32; and Colossians 2:13 it is translated "forgive." The Old Testament example is illustrated in Leviticus 16 where the high priest brought two goats to the Tabernacle of Moses during the great day of atonement. One goat was killed, and its blood was sprinkled upon the Mercy Seat. The other goat was the scapegoat where the High Priest would lay his hands upon the head and confess over him all the iniquities and transgressions of the people (sins). Finally, sending the goat away the animal would bear up all the iniquities and transgressions into a land not inhabited. (Lev 16:21-22) In light of this, carefully read Paul's words in Hebrews. "Wherefore, Jesus also, that He might sanctify the people with His own Blood,

suffered without the gate. Let us go forth therefore unto Him without the camp, bearing His reproach (13:12-13). When the page turned from the Old Covenant to the New Covenant a great problem remained to be solved. It centered around the two words "remission" and "forbearance." How then could God possibly reconcile His holiness and righteousness to His mercy and grace? This problem was gloriously solved in Jesus the Christ as stated in Romans 3:25 as it states that He was "set forth to be a propitiation." Of the 15 words in the Salvation Vocabulary we are discussing here the word "remission" has to do with "SUBTRACTION," whereas all other terms speak of glorious "ADDITION."

6. Redemption: Luke 1:68 says, "Blessed be the Lord God of Israel; for He hath visited and redeemed His people." We can also read Galatians 3:13 where it says, "Christ hath redeemed us from the curse of the Law." Redemption is a 3-fold cord to grasp to understand. 1st it means to pay a ransom price for something or someone. 2nd it means to remove from a slave marketplace. Finally, and the 3rd meaning is to affect a full release.

7. Regeneration: Titus says, "Not by works of righteousness which we have done, but according to His Mercy He saved us, by the washing of regeneration, and renewing of the Holy Ghost." To define this word t means that it is that process whereby God through a second birth imparts to the believing sinner a new nature. (John 1:12-13; 3:3' 1 John 5:1) It is necessary for regeneration to take place because of the corruptness of mankind and the human nature itself. The very fruits of regeneration towards the twice-born believer experiences (1) relationship with other Christians, (2) Jesus, (3) the separated life, (4) the Word of God, and last but not least (5) prayer.

8. Imputation: Here is a word that has been a challenge for many to understand. Romans 4:8 reveals the sincerity of this word in saying, "Blessed is the man to whom the Lord will not impute sin." A simple definition of the word means the act of one person adding something good or bad to the account of another person. In fact, there are three kinds of imputing in the Bible. The 1st one is the imputation of Adam's sin upon the human race. The next is the imputing of the race's sin upon Christ. The third is the imputation of God's righteousness upon the believer's soul.

9. Adoption: In the Book of Galatians (4:4-5) we discover the reality of this word. Adoption is defined as literally the placing of a son. Logically, adoption follows regeneration. So, what is the difference between spiritual adoption and human adoption or civil adoption? We never adopt our own children, do we? However, in the case of God's adoption, He never adopts any other. On the other hand, in comparison, The Father must begin the action leading to the adoption. Both adoptions give an inheritance to the one who previously had none. Also, both adoptions provide a new name to the adoptee or new son.

10. Supplication: Another word for this vocabulary tern in salvation is also a part of prayer, yet it is not prayer of and by itself. Paul's letter to Timothy reveals how serious supplication is, for he ranks it right up there along with prayers, intercessions, and the giving of thanks (1st letter ch.2 verse 1). Paul told the church at Ephesus (6:18) that we should be praying always with all prayer AND supplications in the Spirit. He said the same thing to the church at Philippi (4:6). To define prayer is to say that prayer is in reality "having fellowship with God" It is more than just talking to God. SUPPLICATION is the very essence of the adoption experience because prayer is more than talking "TO" God, but rather talking "WITH" God. The difference between the two is that prayer is that 2-way communication WITH God, while supplication is the boldly pleading for something for someone in sincerity and persistence. It is just like the small child in the check-out line at the grocery store. Have you ever noticed how many different ways the same child asks for the same candy? That is supplication.

11. Justification: Here is a word that for some would think or believe negatively. Job asked the question; how then can man be justified with God? Or How can he be clean that is born of a woman or flesh? Later, Paul, the apostle would answer this question in Romans 5:1, "Therefore being justified by faith,

we have peace with God through our Lord Jesus Christ." We need justification. You see we were placed on trial or an auction block and the highest bidder at the time before Calvary was the devil because man could identify with the devil as man was led by that evil for man's heart was evil. The Judge (GOD) had to bring judgment. Always remember that when a King sits on His throne, He is there to RULE and to REIGN. As the Judge, you do not want to find yourself on the side of evil to experience the due diligence and justice that will be ensued upon your soul. Therefore, Justification can be defined as strong because the Judicial act of God is laid aside or absorbed by the very act of Jesus to change our status from guilty to innocent. Jesus declares thru His Blood upon a cross that we have been restored. Justification is that legal act whereby man's status with God is changed for the good and towards the very end. The very method of justification is located in and through faith (Rom 4:16; 5:1). God receives glory by His grace that He sheds abroad. The ending conclusion or result of justification is the remission of sin's penalty and that the restoration to have relationship with God's Great Divine Favor is met, finalizing that the imputation of Christ's righteousness is just that, final. For example, man justifies the innocent especially if that innocence is realized thru those things that we find innocent. Man justifies on self-merit unlike that of the Savior's.

Watch for Part III on Salvational Vocabulary Words in the July issue of Faith Unlimited!

Central Pacific Rebuilders

IS YOUR STARTER OR ALTERNATOR DEAD?
Give 'em CPR! Central Pacific Rebuilders!

Locations in Wasilla – 907 631 3400 and Anchorage, AK 907 274 9911

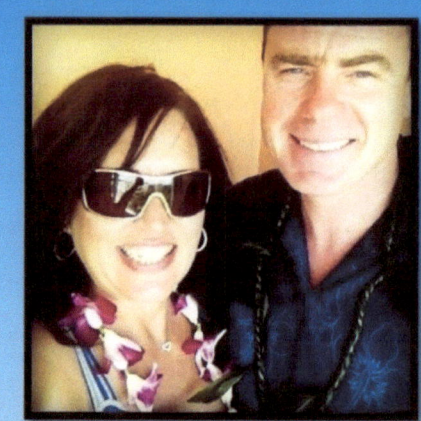

Mike and Genice Fulton, Founders of Central Pacific Rebuilders

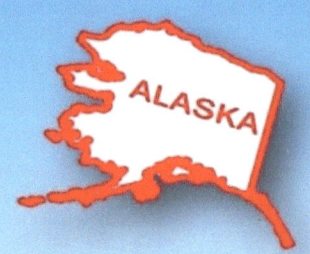

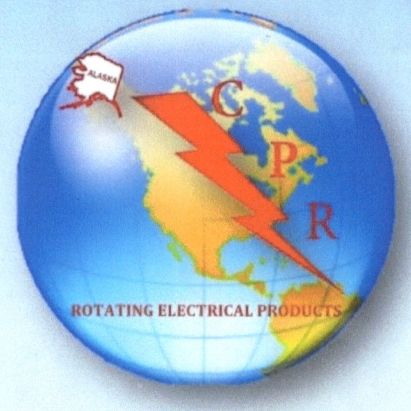

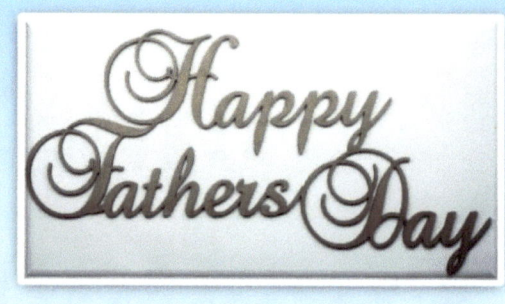

"like" us on Facebook!
Facebook.com/CentralPacificRebuilders
Follow us on Twitter!
@starterman_CPR
www.starterman.com

ONE OF THE HARDEST DECISIONS YOU WILL EVER FACE IS KNOWING WHEN TO TALK AND WHEN TO LISTEN!

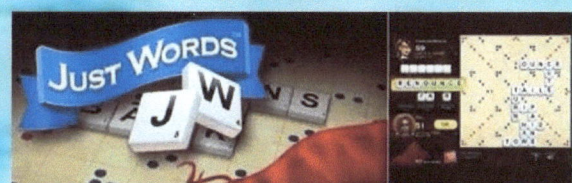

AND ARE THEY "JUST WORDS??"

by: Dewanshu Ahlawat

Choose Your Words Carefully

A person who says whatever he likes usually ends up hearing what he doesn't like. Be tactful. Tact consists of choosing one's words carefully and knowing how far to go. It also means knowing what to say and what to leave unsaid. Talent without tact may not always be desirable. Words reflect attitude. Words can hurt feelings and destroy relationships. More people have been hurt by an improper choice of words than by any natural disaster. Choose what you say rather than say what you choose. That is the correct difference between foolishness and wisdom. Excessive talking does not mean communication. Talk less and say more.

A fool speaks without thinking, a wise man thinks before speaking. Words spoken out of bitterness can cause irreparable damage. The way parents speak to their children in many instances shapes their children's destiny. Let me explain this better with the help of a beautiful story. A farmer slandered his neighbor. Realizing his mistake, he went to the preacher to ask for forgiveness. The preacher told him to take a bag of feathers and drop them in the center of town. The farmer did as he was told. Then the preacher asked him to collect the feathers and put them back in the bag. The farmer tried but could not as the feathers had all blown away. When he returned with the empty bag, the preacher said, "The same thing is true about words. You dropped them rather easily, but you cannot retrieve them. You need to be very careful in choosing your words.

Don't Criticize and Complain

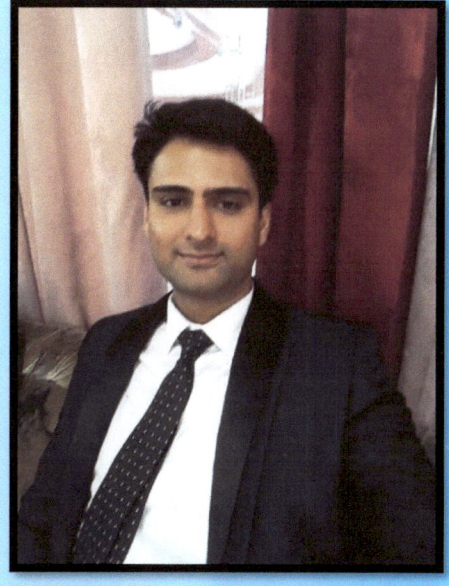

When I talk of criticism, I refer to negative criticism. When a person is criticized, he becomes defensive. A critic is often like a back-seat driver who drives the driver mad. Criticize the behavior not the person, because when we criticize the person, we hurt their self-esteem. The right to criticize comes with the desire to help. As long as the act of criticizing does not give pleasure to the giver, it is okay. When giving criticism becomes a pleasure, it is time to stop. There will always be time when you will be criticized, sometimes justly and sometimes unjustly. The greatest people in the world have been criticized. Justified criticism can be very helpful and should be taken positively as feedback. Some people are complainers. If it is hot, it is too hot. If it is cold, it is too cold. Every day is a bad day for them. They complain even if everything goes right. Why to complain? Because 50% of people do not care if you have a problem and remaining 50% are happy that you have a problem. So, what is the point of complaining? Nothing comes out of it. Rather it becomes a personality trait of that person. Does that mean we should never complain or invite complaints? Not at all. Just like criticism, if done in a positive way, complaints can be very useful. A constructive complaint shows that the complainer cares, and it also gives the receiver of complaints a second chance to rectify himself or herself.

Be a Good Listener

We often read that the art of conversation is dying. Listening shows caring. When you show a caring attitude towards another person, that person feels important. When he feels important, what happens? He is more motivated and receptive to your ideas.

In order to be a good listener:
- Encourage the speaker to talk.
- Ask questions. It shows interest.
- Don't Interrupt.
- Don't change the topic.
- Show understanding and respect.
- Pay attention, concentrate.
- Avoid distractions.
- Listen to feelings and not just words.
- Concentrate on the message and not on the delivery.
- Read the nonverbal communications such as facial expressions, eye contact, body language, and hand movements, etc.

This article is written by Dewanshu Ahlawat, M.Tech and having 26 certifications. By writing this article, I am not teaching you all these points. I am writing to inculcate these valuable points in myself too. I am myself a student of life. I have just finished reading a Motivation Book by an Indian Author Sir ShiV Khera. The words are mine, but inspiration is from his wonderful book. I thought of sharing this wonderful piece of advice with all of you. I would like to express my thanks to Editor in Chief Mrs Faye G Hanshew and Sir Bill Hanshew for publishing my article in their amazing magazine. See you all readers in the next month edition of "FAITH UNLIMITED."

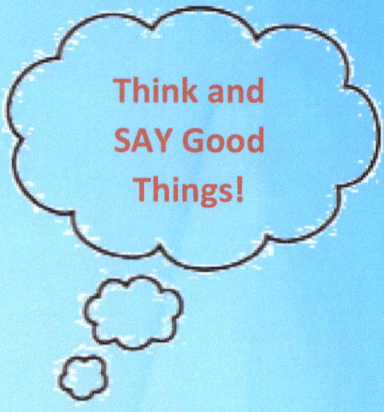

Think and SAY Good Things!

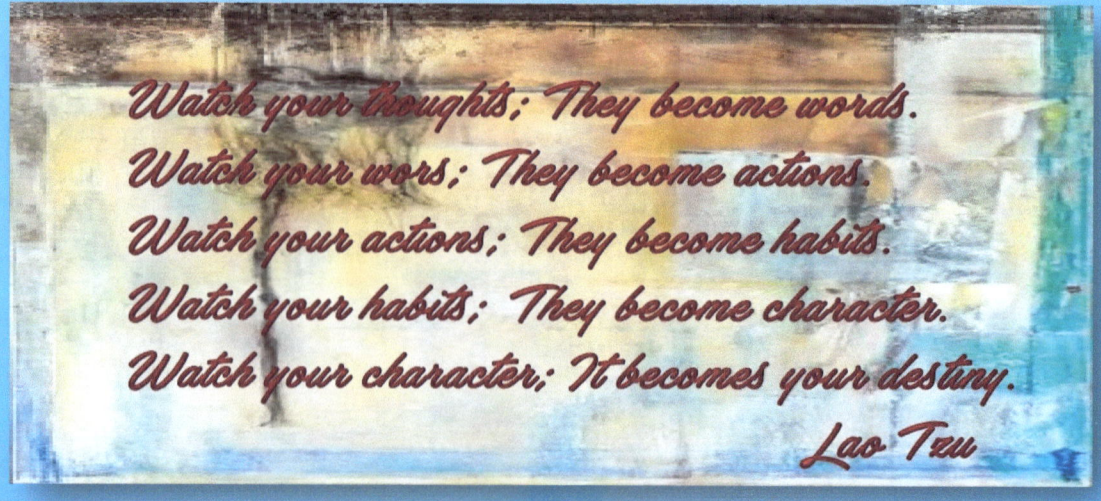

Watch your thoughts; They become words.
Watch your wors; They become actions.
Watch your actions; They become habits.
Watch your habits; They become character.
Watch your character; It becomes your destiny.

Lao Tzu

HOPE OF LIFE CHURCH AND MINISTRIES

PROJECTS:

1. Orphanage for parentless children
2. School for needy and poor Christian Children
3. Sewing Training Center for widows and needy girls

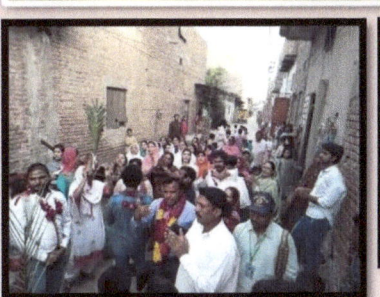
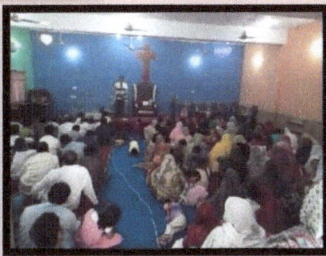
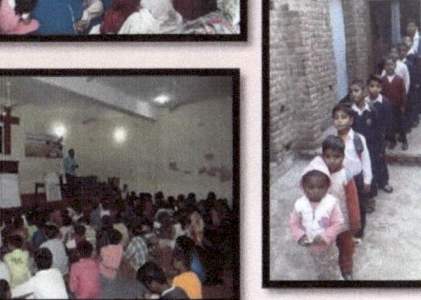
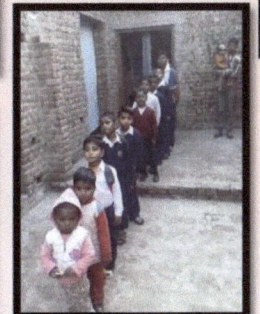
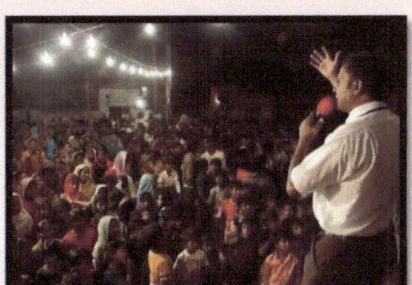

Pastor Saleem Shahid

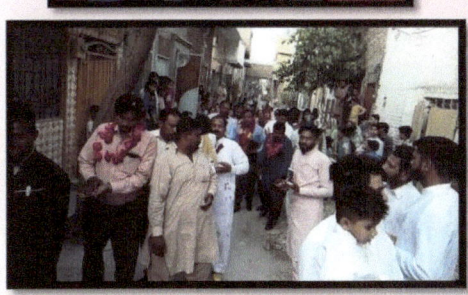
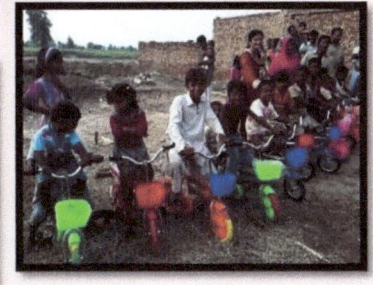
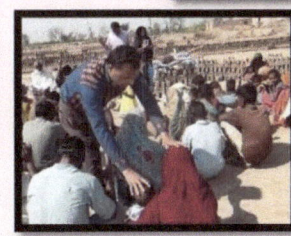
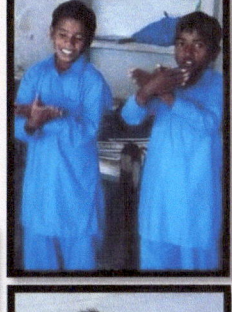
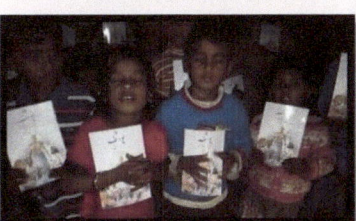
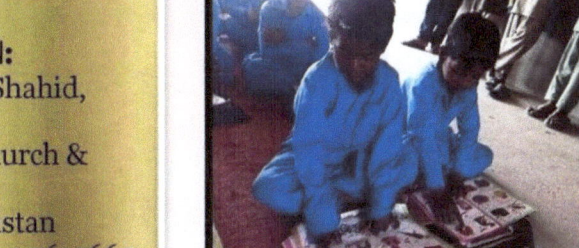
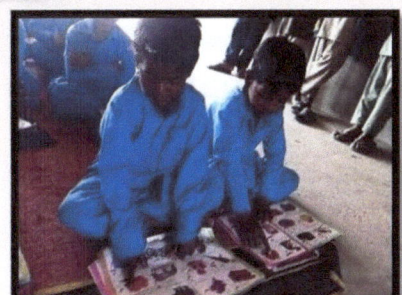
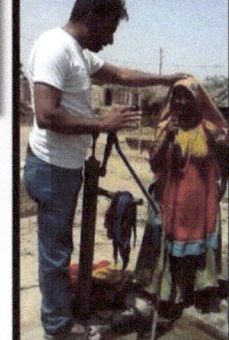
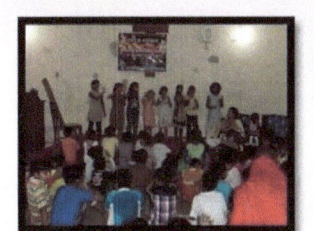

CONTACT INFORMATION:
Pastor Saleem Shahid, Chairman
Hope of Life Church & Ministries
Faisalabad Pakistan
Mobile : +92 300 7615665
Email: saleem_rehmat2000@hotmail.com
Skype: saleem.rehmat2

Happy Father's Day!

KENYACARE

A Farming Community caring for the poor in Northwestern Kenya

James 1:27 – Care for Orphans and Widows

PROJECTS:

1. To provide improved shelter
2. To provide Clothing
3. To provide Food
4. To provide Education

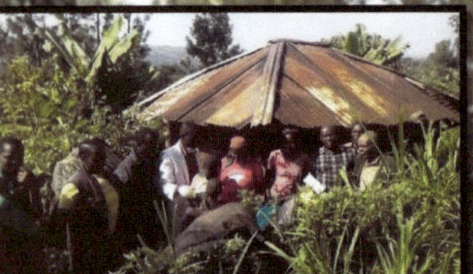
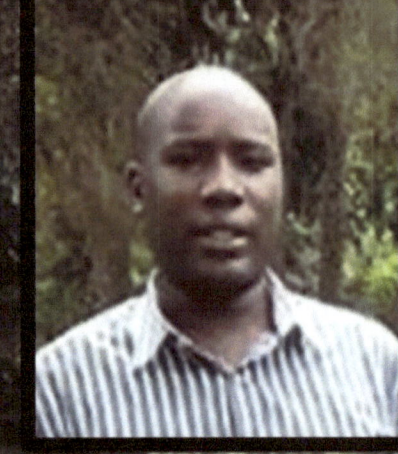
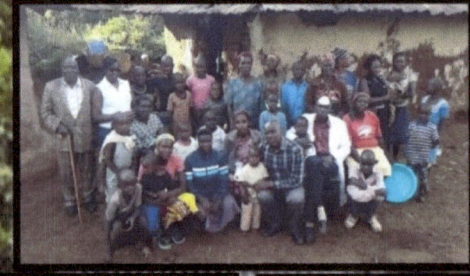
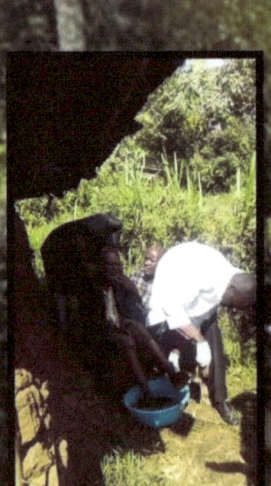
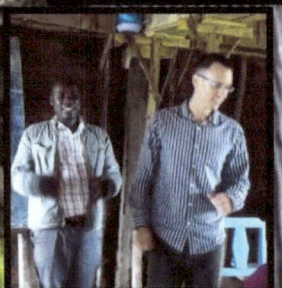
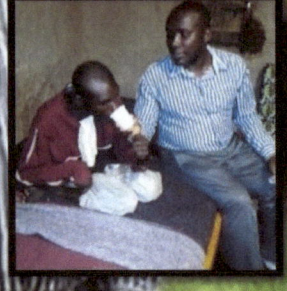
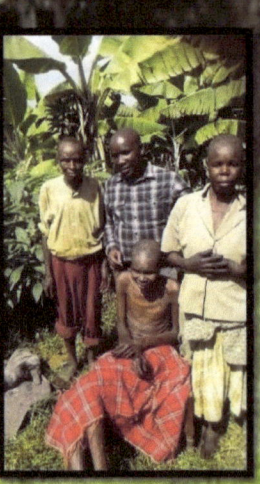
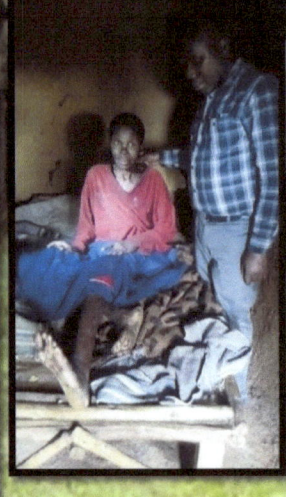

KENYACARE...This is exactly what Dennis Torori does in Kenya. The Kenyacare Team, under the leadership of Director Dennis Torori, goes around to the villages and helps care for the people with Education, Food, Clothing, and Medicine. He raises herbs to buy medicine for the people. Now he is also making honey, soap, wax, shampoo, and candles. He is hoping to provide some improvements to many shelters that need updating, along with providing Education, Clothing and Food for the many people.

If you have even a little extra to help Dennis, he will appreciate it very much. He loves the people of Kenya, and does his very best to help them. Please be a part of this great work in Kenya!

Faye Hanshew
Publisher of Faith Unlimited

Contact Information:

Coordinator Dennis Torori,
Address:
40502-132 Nyansiongo,
Nyamira County, Kenya
Email: tororid@gmail.com
Skype: dennistorori1
Phone: +254725907179
Website: www.kenyacare.org

The Father-Heart of God

by Pastor Jo Bruns

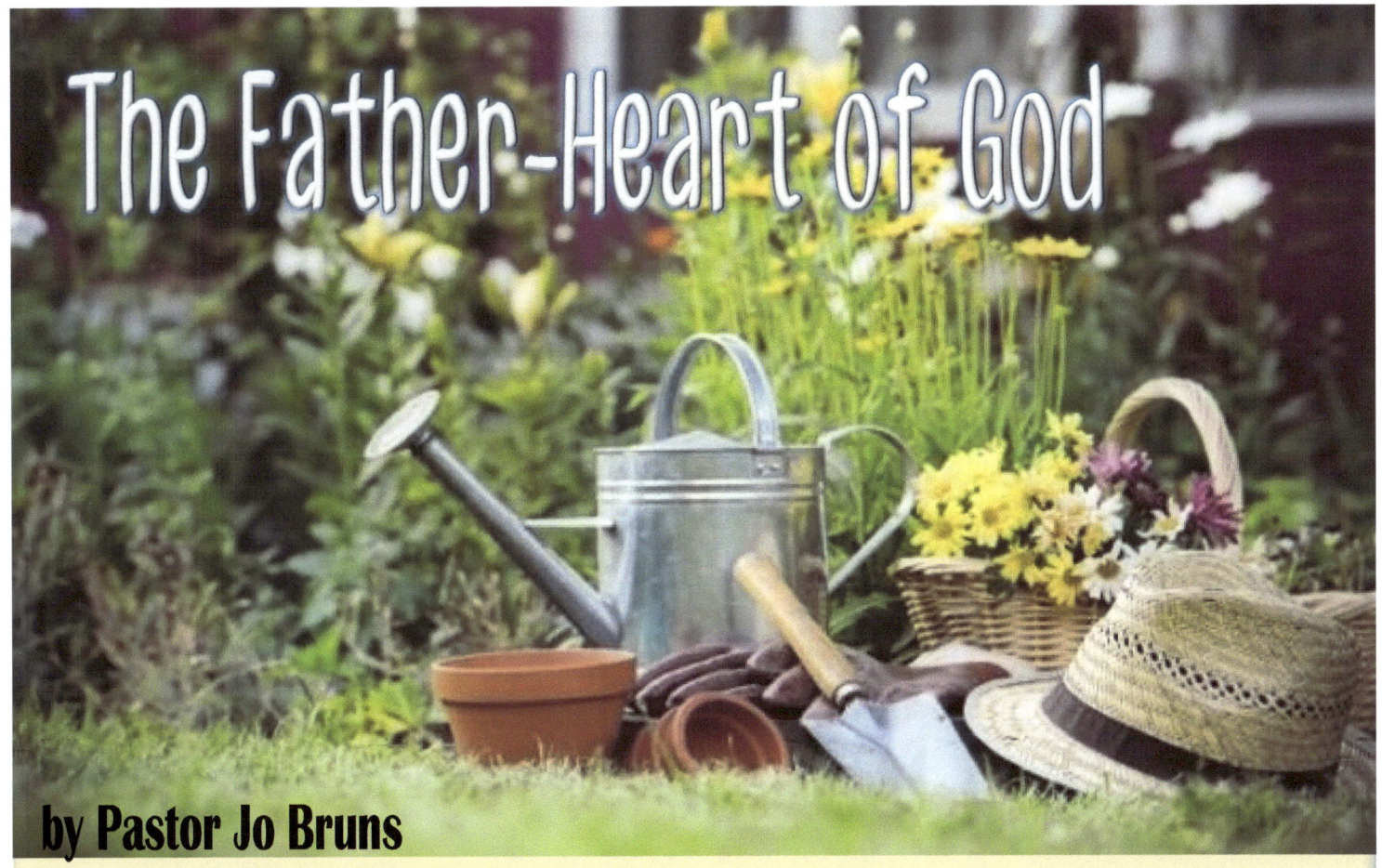

"The Spirit you received does not make you slaves so that you live in fear again; rather the Spirit you received was brought about by your adoption to sonship. And by Him, we cry, "Abba Father." Romans 8:15 (NIV)

June is known for many things—the promise of warm, sunny summer days, the planting of flowers and vegetable gardens, Father's Day and barbeques, and for its many June weddings. Love restores and renews our weary souls, especially after harsh winters and rainy springs; and it brings hope and healing to our lives. So, what better time to remind ourselves of the greatest love of all—the love of our Savior.

As I sought the Lord in prayer and in meditating on the Word as I prepared for this month's message, I kept hearing in my spirit the word, "Love." In particular--Our Heavenly Father's Love and His heart towards those He loves.

Now, I admit, there are some who have never known a father's love. Some don't even know who their father might be. We can attest to that with the billboard's which read, "Who's your daddy?" encouraging DNA testing. Some don't know their father due to an untimely death or divorce. Still, others may have had a very abusive father or step-father who didn't express the example of what a father's love toward their child might be. Because of this, many struggle with the idea that God could love them unconditionally and without reservation.

Yet, I can assure you that God's love is perfect—without flaws and is genuine. You don't have to perform for Him to be loved and accepted, because He loves you unconditionally. Once you grasp hold of God's love for you and catch a glimpse of what His love is like, your life will be transformed and radically changed. In Ephesians

3:16-18, the Apostle Paul writes, "I pray that from His glorious, unlimited resources He will empower you with inner strength through His Spirit. Then Christ will make His home in your hearts as you trust in Him. Your roots will grow down into God's love and keep you strong. And may you have the power to understand, as all God's people should, how wide, how long, how high, and how deep His love is."

As I studied on the love of God, I came to understand this: God loves us with an everlasting love. He will never leave us or forsake us. In fact, as much as we often say, "We need God," the truth of the matter is "He wants us." He created us in His image in the very beginning because He wanted fellowship with those He created. We, as believers in Jesus Christ, have the same DNA as our Heavenly Father. And, like a good Father, He will sometimes discipline us, as needed, in order to help us grow. And, at other times, He will step back to allow us to go our own way to learn from our experiences. Yet, He encourages us, calls to us, and loves us even when we are far from Him. He stands with arms wide open waiting for us to come running and to jump into His arms and climb upon His lap like any small child might do with their natural father. "I have loved you with an everlasting love," He says in Jeremiah 31:3, "That is why I have continued to be faithful to you."

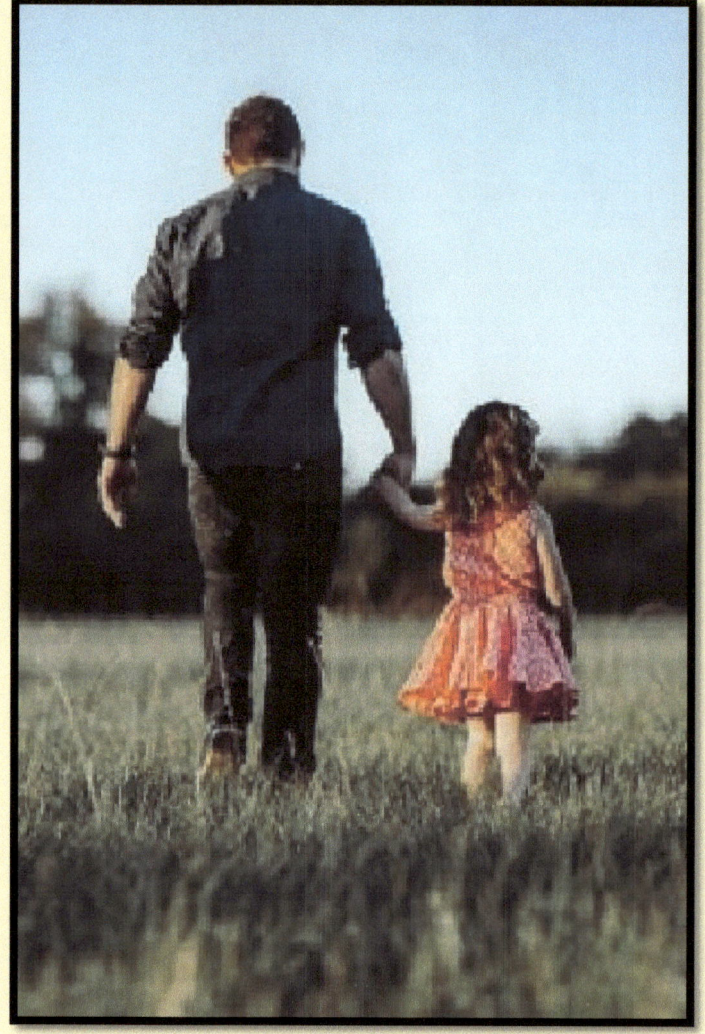

He stands at a distance, sometimes, just waiting for us to come to Him so that He can wrap us in His arms and lavish us with His love. Yet, His heart is torn because of how we often reject or push away His love and affection toward us. Or that we just don't even have a clue as to how much He truly loves us. Yet He truly wants to have that intimate Father/Son or Father/Daughter relationship with each one of us. He has no favorites because we are all His favorites.

So, as I close, I want to leave you with this--a love letter from God's Heart to Yours:

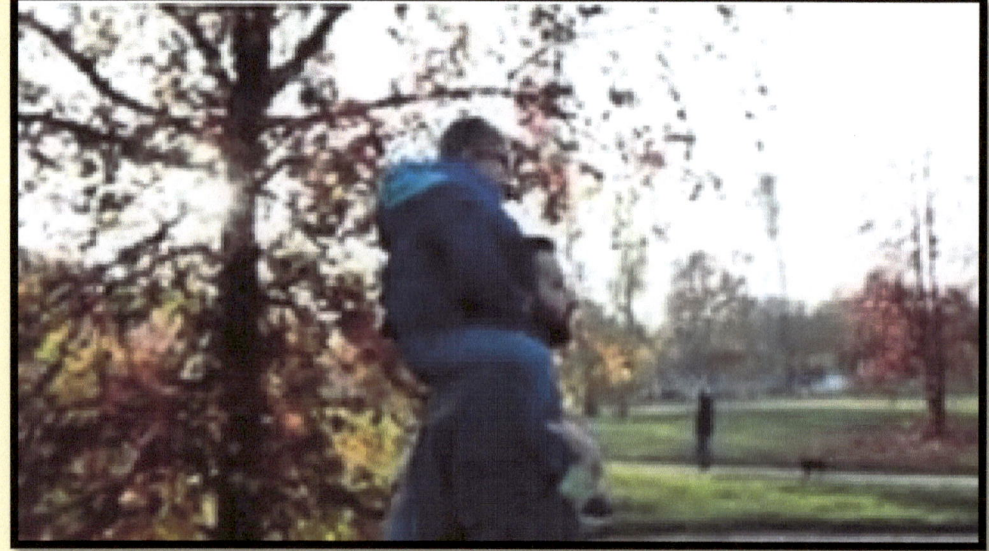

My Beloved Child,

Even before you were born, I knew you and I danced the day you were born. I know the number of hairs on your head and I know the desires of your heart. I have laughed with you and I've seen and wiped away your tears. I have led you by the hand and taught you to walk. I have led you along with my ropes of kindness and love and have kept your feet from slipping and falling. I have sung songs of deliverance over you. But, my heart is broken and torn, at times, as I see that you've rejected my love and have looked for it in all the wrong places. I am not in the wind or the whirlwind. Nor will you find Me in that bottle of pills that you choose to take to ease your pain. I know you yearn for and desire love, but it's not in the cheap sex of your lovers. Oh, child, I so want to take away all your hurt and pain and turn your ashes into something beautiful. You see, I have loved you with an everlasting love and I will remain faithful to you. My spirit is as close as a whisper, if you'd only listen. But, I knew, long ago, that sin would rule your heart. That's why I sent My son, Jesus, to you to help you find the way for you to come home to Me. Yes, while you were deep in sin and stuck in the miry clay, I made a way of escape for you so that you would know my love. My Beloved Child, please come home. Grace awaits you. Forgiveness awaits you. Love awaits you; for I am Love. I am all you've ever really needed. I will do exceedingly, abundantly, above all you've ever dreamed or imagined. So, remember this, come home, My Child for My love awaits.

Love, Your Daddy

TRANSFORMATION LIFE CHURCH – KENYA
T.L.C. NAIROBI
A MINISTRY OF DIVINE INTERVENTION GLORY MINISTRIES

PROJECT:
- Raising $1,000 to finish the land payment
- Feeding the Orphan children
- School books for the Orphan children
- Shoes for the Orphan Children

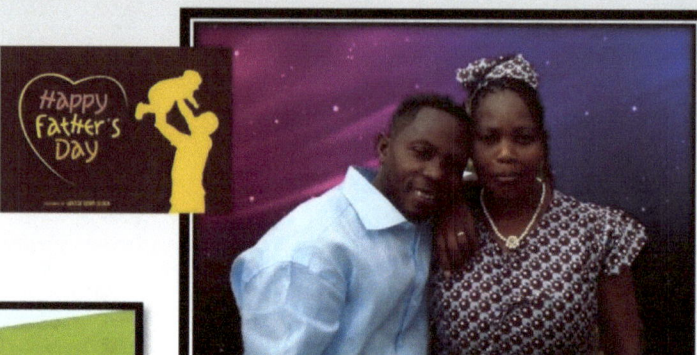

Pastor Bosco Munyu

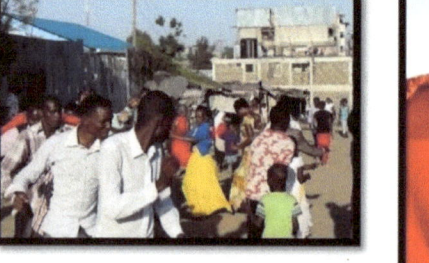
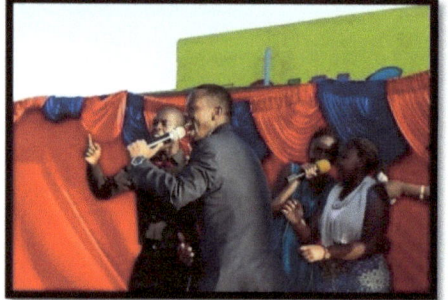
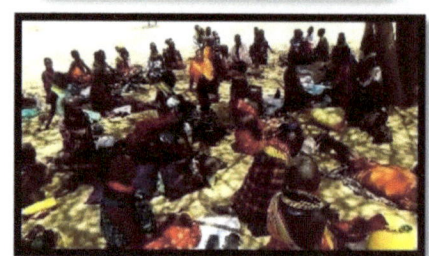
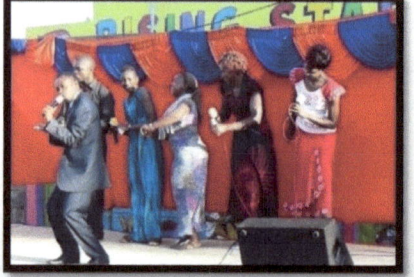
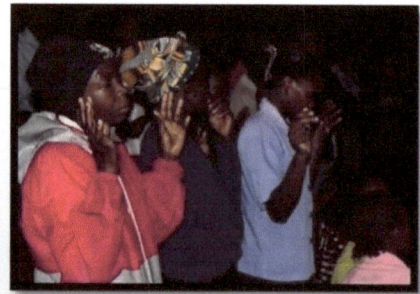
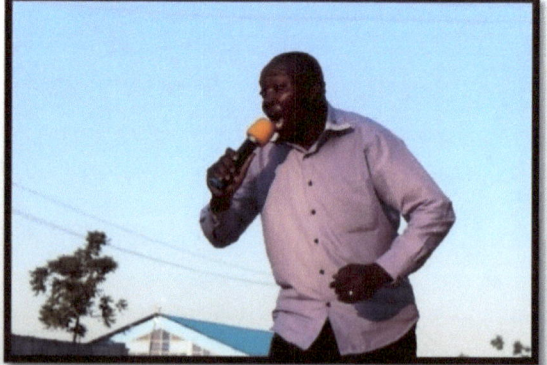
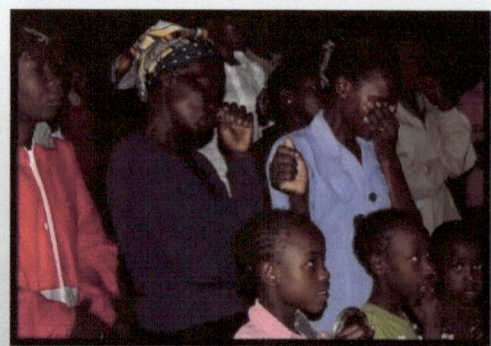

THANK YOU FOR YOUR HELP
GOD BLESS YOU!

CONTACT INFORMATION:
Pastor Bosco Munyu
BOX 37780-00100
NAIROBI-KENYA,
TEL +245-714294407
     +254-726904555

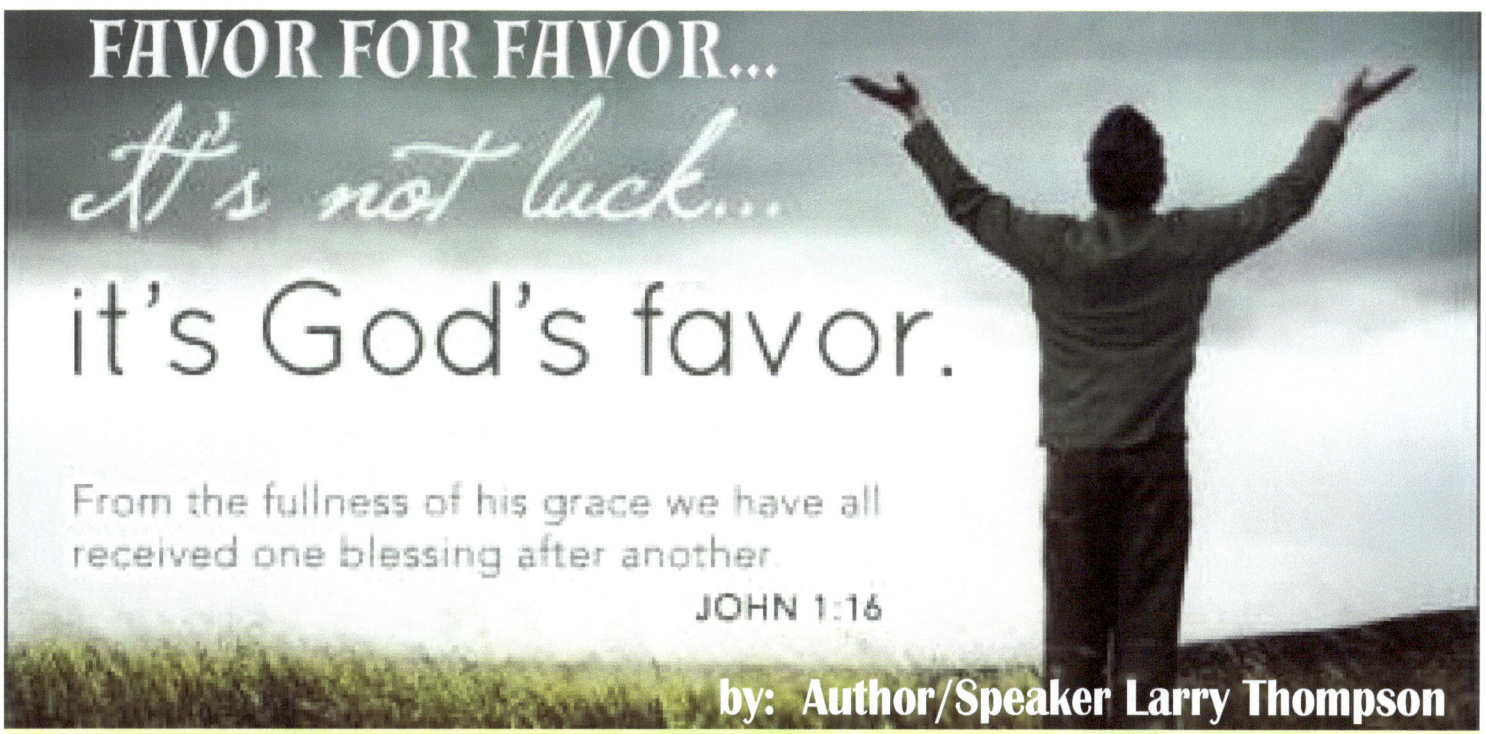

FAVOR FOR FAVOR...
It's not luck... it's God's favor.

From the fullness of his grace we have all received one blessing after another.
JOHN 1:16

by: Author/Speaker Larry Thompson

There is something you want, there is something He wants. He has provided all that you will ever need by giving you the same glory He had with the Father. Your favor is that He has granted you direct access to His glory which is being manifested through every revelation by the Holy Spirit. These kingdom secrets are being revealed by this knowledge of the glory. It should be noted that He wants to give more than we are ready to receive. That first level of understanding how to operate with Him in His glory comes through the wisdom found in Scripture, which the Holy Spirit made known to you. The Holy Spirit is following the very pattern that Jesus spoke, concerning the secrets of the Kingdom. He declared that nothing is hidden that shall not be revealed. We grow from glory to glory by revelation. When the wisdom and revelation become our experiences, then the knowledge of the glory is permanent residency. It is this intimate relationship that the Father decided that we would enjoy all along.

The glimpses from Scripture are as training modules by the Holy Spirit to teach us His ways, His truth, and His life. They are specialized as a private tutor giving unique lessons to each of us individually. We are given the opportunity to grow and perfect every revelation given so that the end result for anyone, is that we know how to listen and follow the voice of the Holy Spirit and understand how to work with Him in His glory. The two become one.

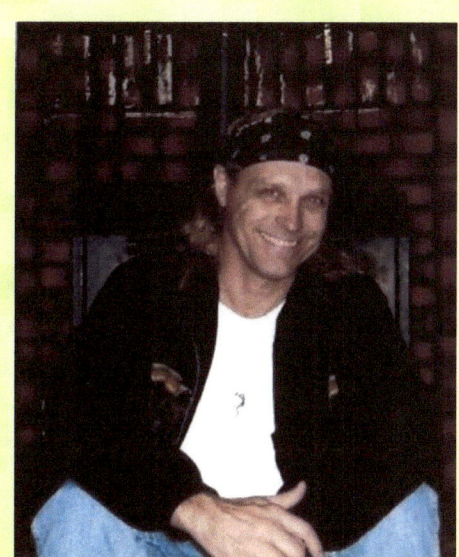

Consider the story of the wedding in Cana. Jesus displayed His first miracle, His first sign as the glory was being manifested through a man. Whenever His glory is manifested many things shift in the spirit realm. In this case, many believed in Jesus. The awakening of His glory is what manifested. The reality before that was only words and ideas, but the manifestation of His glory solidified all things true in the spiritual realm. Mary states that they ran out of wine. The implication is a request to have more wine for the rest of the days of the feast which would have been a week long–this was only the third day of the feast. That fact by itself is also a prophetic truth concerning the complete plan of the Father. Every detail when understood through the Father's eyes are insights into all things He is doing. Jesus stated many times that He only did what He saw the Father doing, and He only said what He heard the Father saying.

Jesus replied to His mother, "Woman, what does your concern have to do with Me? My hour has not yet come." This question and statement reveal the heart of the Father. There is something that the Father wants, there is something that we want, like Mary, the immediate concerns all around us. The Father has His eyes on eternity, hence the words, ...My time has not yet come." Every covenant has two parts, that which is our part, and in this case that which is the Father's part. The language for covenant is revealed by both. This would not be unlike any mathematical problem where there are unseemly parts of the equation that do not necessarily look like the other side of the equation. The equal sign by definition makes the two separate sides of the equation equal. It could become missed in the language what Mary states, and the language what Jesus states. From our perspective, there is no way that the water should have turned to wine.

Our simple answer many times is too shallow to give greater clarity as to what just happened. It is also the main reason many times we do not understand our own answers to prayer. It seems hit and miss most of the time as though it were only a faith accident, but we have no way of understanding the network of how things manifested. That is the great revelation of this knowledge of the glory—it reveals all things. That which was hidden is now being revealed. This is a present tense experience in His glory. This is the Father's grand purpose for the church; that they would come up higher, operating in the heavenly realm and exercising authority over all the principalities and powers.

Mary's request for more wine, and her statement, "Whatever He says to you, do it," make up the language of covenant, what she says, and what Jesus says, the two become one, glory is manifested. Jesus did not ask the Father anything; it is not written He gave thanks and the water multiplied. He does not even touch the water Himself. Everything about this first miracle is a training module from the Holy Spirit on a greater scale to teach us how to operate in the very same glory He had deposited in us. Jesus spoke to the servants, "Fill the waterpots with water," and then He told them, "Draw some out now, and take it to the master of the feast." Jesus said nothing else, and only these words. These words coupled with what Mary spoke are the very words that manifested His glory. If you accelerated ahead to chapter 15 of John's gospel, Jesus states these words for us, "No longer do I call you servants, for a servant does not know what his master is doing; but I have called you friends, for all things that I heard from My Father I have made known to you. By this, the language of heaven has been transferred with these rich treasures to us now. Whatever we ask and declare will be manifested. It will be done now according to what we say.

To abide in Jesus and His words abiding in us, is the sovereign decision of the Father. This glorifies the Father when we declare His words. It glorifies Jesus when the Holy Spirit declares to us the language of heaven. The same stream from the throne of glory began with the Father. All that the Father has, has been given to Jesus, and all that Jesus received, it is now being declared to us. This is the same stream coming from the throne. Now it is our turn, declaring all that the Holy Spirit is declaring to us. This proves that we are no longer servants, but friends, His disciples, displaying the knowledge of the glory and manifesting much fruit in all that we say and declare. This glorifies the Father, that we are walking in the same glory as Jesus' earth-walk, and that we are being transformed from one level of glory to the next.

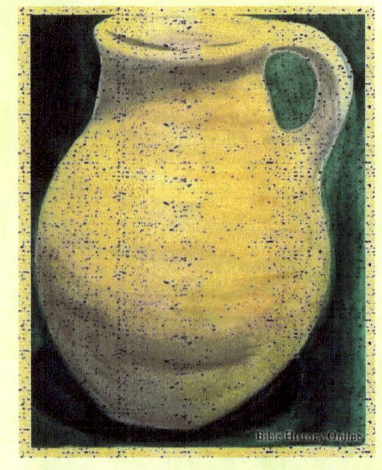

DIE NO MORE

by: Ernest Kweku Nanor

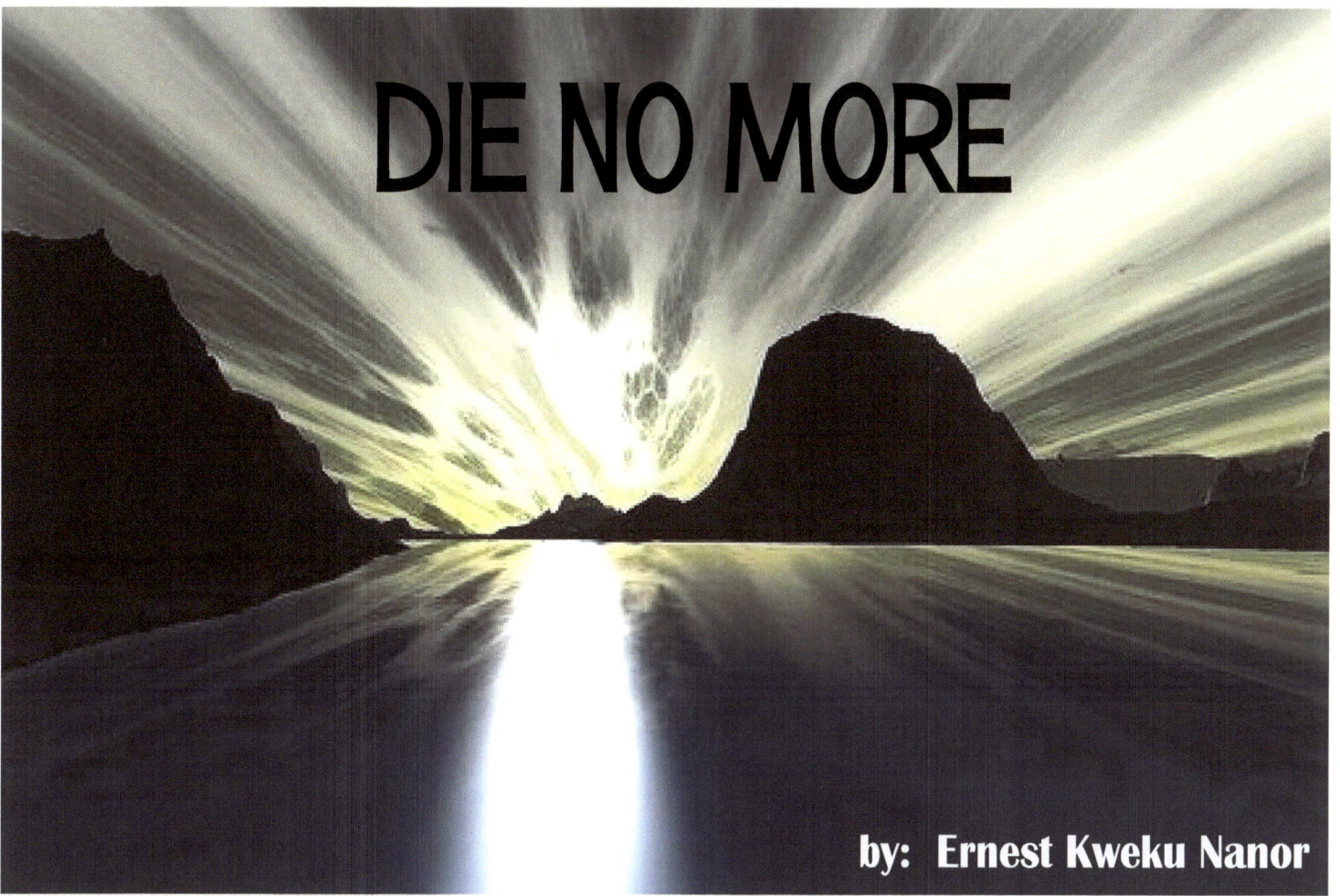

"[1] And you were dead in the trespasses and sins [2] in which you once walked, following the course of this world, following the prince of the power of the air, the spirit that is now at work in the sons of disobedience–" (Ephesians 2:1-2, ESV)

Trespasses and sins:

In the book of Ezekiel, in the thirty-seventh chapter, the writer presented to us some unspeakable inspirations are beyond human imagination. One of the inspirations was about the valley of the dry bones that reflected the lost hope of Israel at a time they were in exile and expecting to be freed, but never knew how to go about it.

In like manner, all human-efforts have faded away, the sun has been darkened, the moon has ceased to give its light, meaning that the stars have fallen, and the powers of Heaven has been shaken! Anytime the scriptures spoke of death, many other words were used to represent it, and some profound and unthinkable ones are words such as trespasses and sin.

Where there are many freedoms, we also fine many boundaries and when people's actions or behaviors crosses those boundaries, we refer those as trespasses; but sin were considered the transgression of the Law.

One way the gospel tries to discourage trespasses and sins within the parameters of the gospel is the definition, endowments, and the institution of specialized gift-ministries in the body of Christ to benefit the whole body.

A clear definition gives the meaning, the powers, and the work of the Apostle, Prophet, Evangelist, Pastor and Teacher to ensure the unity of faith within the mainstream of the body. This also shows the differences by the way each gift operates, such as prophecy, ministry, teaching, exhortation, giving, ruling, and showing mercy; but these gifts also manifest depending on the will of God for each of them.

Like, the valley of dry bones that was revealed to Ezekiel the Prophet, many of these spiritual gifts today are dead and buried by the mass number of people in the Church, either due to failure to recognize their gifts, or a failure to utilize their spiritual gifts.

If I am not doing what I am supposed to do in the body to enable it to function properly, then it is either because I am weak, sick, or dead. If I am sick, it affects the whole body not just me. It is just as the scripture says, that a little leaven or corruption leaveneth the whole lamp. Therefore, if one weeps, all weep; and if one rejoices, all rejoices. The reason is because we are all interconnected to through one body, one baptism, one Spirit and Lord. In the natural sense if people are given many tasks to do, they are given those tasks according to their abilities (Eph 3:20).

In Mathew 25, we read a passage about a man who gave talents to his servant's according to their abilities. In Luke 16, we see that when people are dishonest with the few, there is no way they will be given much. But if they are honest with the few, in the end they receive much.

There are many people who have completed training in universities and colleges and with excellent knowledge and skills in entrepreneurship. But only a few of these have been able to set up their own businesses, living as successful and responsible adults.

In the same way, many Apostles, Prophets, Evangelists, Pastors, and Teachers have been trained in a well-equipped Bible University, having excellent knowledge of their callings and giftings. But only a few of them have been able to successfully come out with innovative ideas that will give nourishment to the entire body of Christ.

In some cases, it is even the people with little or no educational backgrounds who show promising abilities, using their spiritual-gifts or educational qualifications in a way that gives nourishment, strength, and opportunities to the literate. The effect will spread to the majority of people, focusing themselves on duties that are not their duties; and boundaries that are not their boundaries. This causes a whole lot of problems in the main stream; such as envyings, strife, jealousies, divisions, and chaos; which in the natural is not supposed to be so for a people who have been rescued from the power of darkness and brought into the marvelous light of Jesus Christ (1 Peter 2:9-10).

If a person is not dead to trespasses, then it is as a result of sin; just as the bible states categorically that the wages of sin is death, but the Gift of God is eternal life through Jesus Christ our Lord, Amen (Rom 6:23).

Ernest Kweku Nanor - Author of the book, "Revealing Jesus"

THE DEEPER LIFE

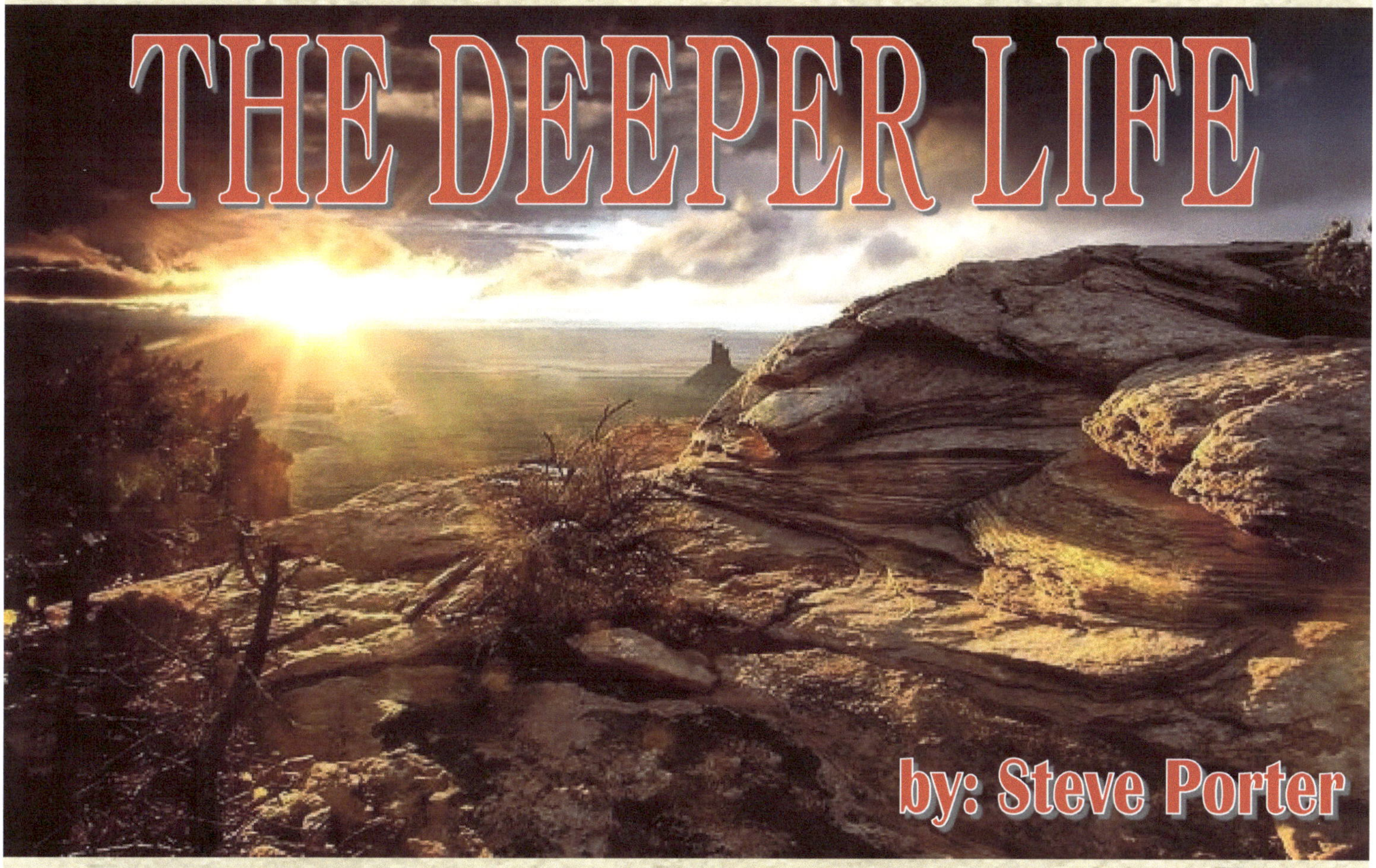

by: Steve Porter

"For many are called, but few are chosen."
Matthew 22:14

In every generation, there are a few rare individuals who break free from mediocrity and apathy. These trailblazers are hungry for God and yield their lives to follow hard after Him. They yearn for something deeper and more meaningful than just a surface relationship with the Savior.

We know from Scripture that "wide is the road that leads to destruction and narrow is the way that leads to life." Hell's highway is wide and broad with people standing shoulder to shoulder, unknowingly edging toward the very edge of the abyss. But there is also a narrow road that leads to life, and if you were to sit under a tree beside the road and watch you would notice that only every so often does anyone pass that way.

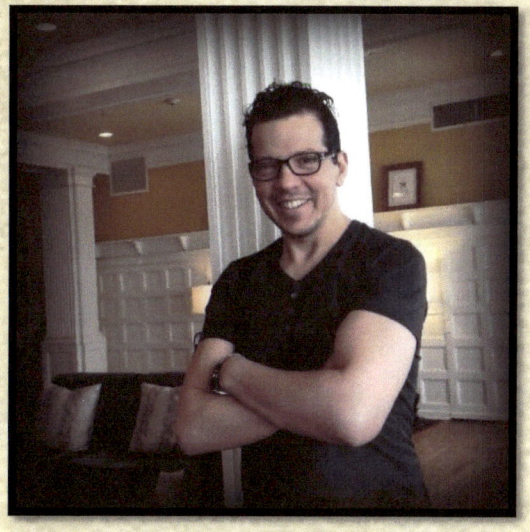

There is also within the body of Christ a broader path called "status quo." Many believers are on this road, saved, with heaven as their final destination, but they fail to seek God's highest or best for their lives. Along this path, there is also a narrow gate that leads a few of us down a path far less traveled. On this path are many twists and turns with bumps and awkward places that require a leap of faith to continue. This is the road called "sacrifice." It is a long walk down this unpopular and lonely road, and few want to go there.

On the road called "status quo," travelers are content with what they've always had. They are enamored by the "blessings" of God. They seek Him for what He can do for them and become spiritually satisfied with the gifts of His hands. They desire a life of ease, comfort, and simplicity. They avoid those who preach about "carrying a cross" or "denying self." It is far easier to seek a popular, "feel good" message.

A rare few travel the path called "sacrifice" and are not content merely to follow the multitudes down a crowded highway. For these saints the only place of deep satisfaction is in His manifest presence, where they can actually touch His face and feel His heartbeat. They're absolutely convinced that He is the only One worth pursuing! They have a kingdom mindset and see things in light of eternity rather than being consumed only by what they see and hear. They cry out with passion, "Jesus I want the deeper life found only in you."

So what does it mean to live the deeper life? It means walking a road far less-traveled where consecration, holiness, humility, intimacy, devotion, and sacrifice are treasured-- where its travelers would rather invest themselves in pleasing God than in pleasing man. It is a place where the Lord rules and reigns in their hearts and they realize that crowns aren't simply given as souvenirs but are earned. Where taking up the cross and following hard after God, though difficult, still brings deep contentment to the soul—and is its own reward. To them pleasing God means everything.

A life of sacrifice and devotion is a virtue, a sweet fragrance that actually scents the throne room and blesses the heart of God. To be perfectly frank, anything less leaves us all feeling empty and dissatisfied. It is not good enough to think ourselves devout because of the number of prayers we pray. If we go home from church and are arrogant and angry toward those we say we love, we are only deceiving ourselves. Spiritual maturity must be more than just a desire or an intention--it must be walked out.

We often fill our lives with empty things and shallow pursuits gradually growing weaker and colder in our souls until we have finally had enough. At that point, a hunger from deep within is born, and we rise up and say, "I'm desperate for more of God!"

Why does it take so long to realize our desperate state and seek the cure? Because it's tough to face the truth we often conceal, even from ourselves—that the old way just doesn't cut it anymore. When the Holy Spirit shows us how weak and wayward we are, we are then humbled and can only cry out with deep hunger for a fresh encounter with the living God, and nothing else will do. In fact, we feel like we'll die without it. It's only at the place where we will settle for nothing less that we are truly ready to go deep with

God.

But be warned. Going hard after God will offend others. It is inevitable--the moment you press into God, Christian friends will show up with "words of encouragement" that are actually ordained by the enemy, designed to quench your fire and stifle the deep hunger inside you. And make no mistake about it, if you act on their words they will lead you back through that narrow gate and onto same old wide way. Better to lose a friend than to miss out on the incredible treasures of the Spirit of God.

And while you may offend those close to you by going hard after God He is pleased and excited by the deep hunger in your heart. That's why you must silence the conflicting voices around you, of both humans and spirits--that urge you to settle for less than God's best. In order to go deep, you must determine in your heart to march to the beat of a different drummer leaving others behind who are not willing to walk the road of sacrifice.

Are you determined enough to arrest God's attention—to say you won't let go until you've pressed in? Are you tired of standing on the sidelines, a mere spectator while the passionate pass you by? Get desperate enough today to press in. Cry out with all your heart, refusing to settle for anything less than God's best. Get hungry for the deeper things of God, moving beyond the status quo to touch His very heart.

Going hard after God will mean loving God not just in word but also in deed. Sweet surrender is the first step to empowerment and the anointing that comes only when we refuse to settle for anything less than serving God with all our hearts, souls, minds and strength. It is hard to convince our finite minds that carrying a cross can bring peace and contentment, but because it is by His strength that we accomplish anything, He gets the glory, and we are filled up in the process.

He is the sweet master, and in order to please Him, we need only adore Him on this narrow path, even without fully understanding it all. By walking the path of sacrifice, we finally realize that we can never become mature without first dying to the old selfish lifestyles that demand more and are never satisfied. In dying to our old man, we become that fully developed "new man" that God intended—something that could never happen otherwise. As we walk down the narrow path of sacrifice, He accomplishes His grand design for our lives. We become reliant on Him, and He frees us from self by revealing our weaknesses by the power of the Holy Spirit. An intense desperation is created by the emptiness we find in all earthly things, which hold little appeal at that point. We discover the doorway to the deeper life by first being discontent with a shallow, egocentric existence.

The natural man would love to go deep in Christ and his pure love at no cost, but it is only his excessive self-love and pride that acts so childish and demanding in the first place. And while God's fatherly heart takes no joy in seeing us struggle He knows the road of sacrifice brings about steadfastness and meekness, purifying our motives and intentions to the point where we are worthy to feel His deepest heart cries and carry His message of love to a lost and dying world.

Take heart, precious friend, when bearing the cross down the narrow and winding road of sacrifice, as you anticipate the joy that comes with pressing in. As you go hard after God, let me encourage you. You have set out on a journey of divine proportions, determined to settle for nothing less than touching the very heart of God, and I guarantee that in that place is fullness of joy, where you will find that He is altogether lovely and everything you ever wanted.

Steve Porter

Rochester, New York

www.findrefuge.tv

Steve and his wife Diane founded "Refuge Ministries". Steve is a regular contributor to many prophetic publications including the Elijah List, Spirit Fuel, and the Identity Network. His writings have been read worldwide by hundreds of thousands of people. He also has been interviewed by the Trinity Broadcasting Network and a few other TV programs. Steve's books, articles, and videos have touched countless lives around the world. The Porters reside near Rochester, NY.

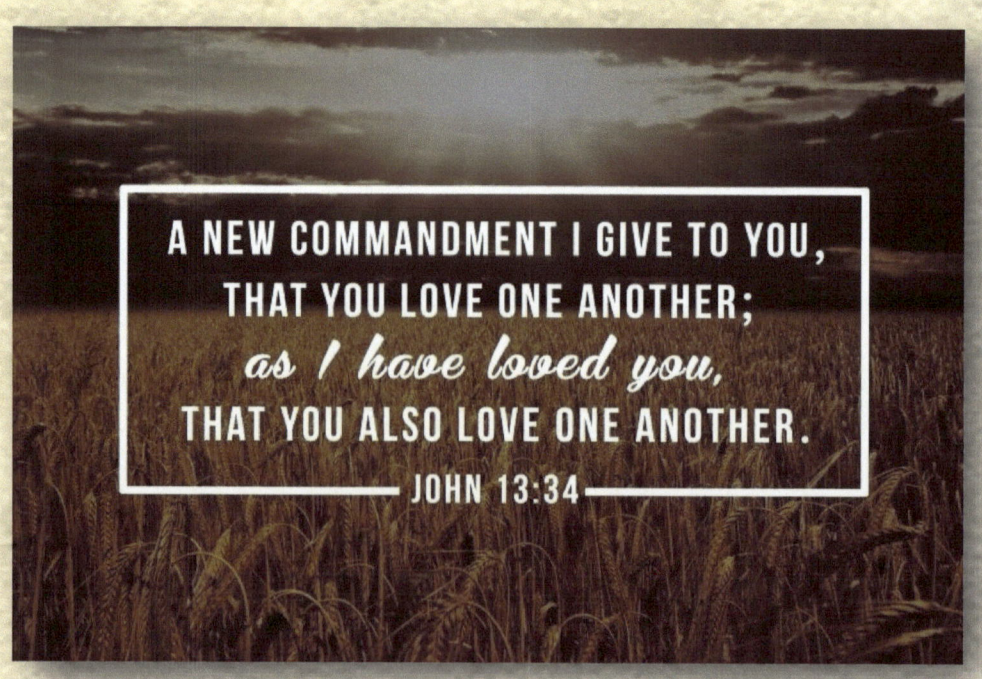

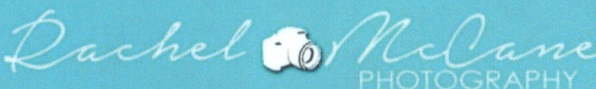

573-308-6504
 www.facebook.com/rachel.mccanephotography

FAMILY

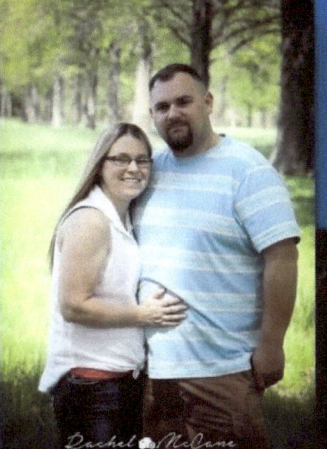
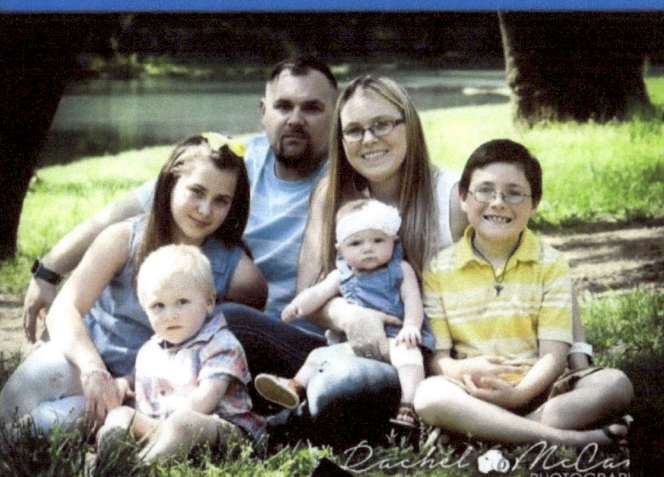
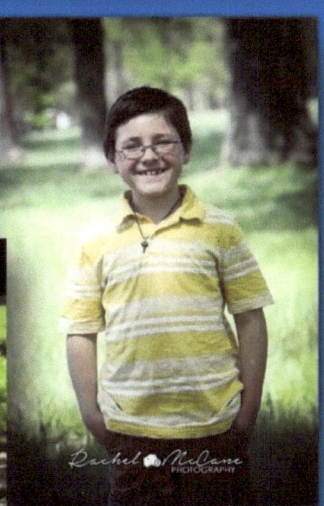
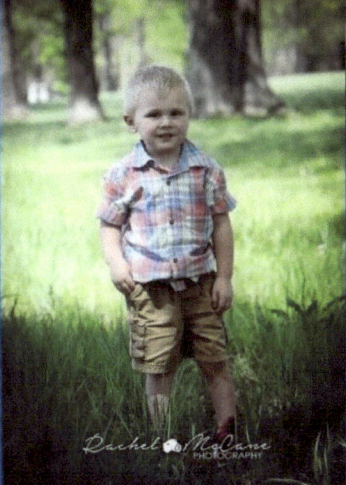
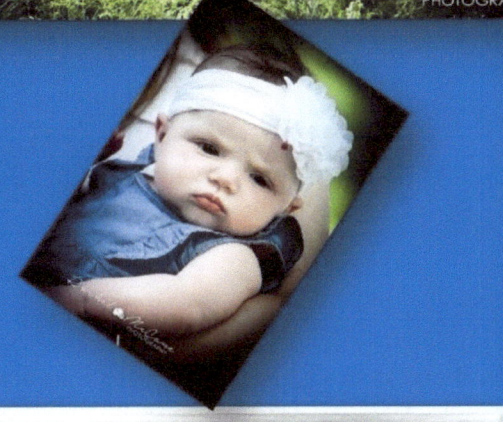
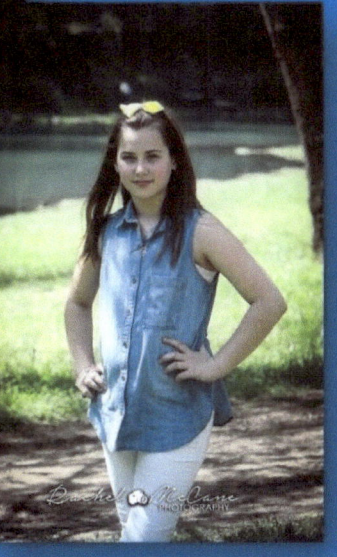
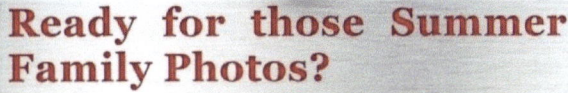

Ready for those Summer Family Photos?

Contact Rachel today! She can make your memories last!

15949 Highway A Vichy, MO 65580
573-201-9981

Email: flying_dragon_tkd@hotmail.com

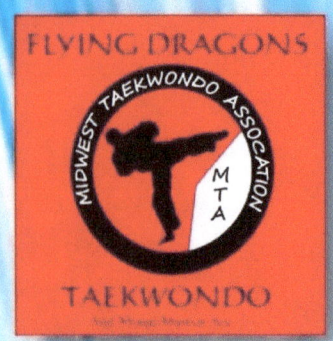

The Flying Dragons Taekwondo and Mixed Arts Training Center
A place of honor, loyalty, and respect.
Not to mention great times, and a family atmosphere.

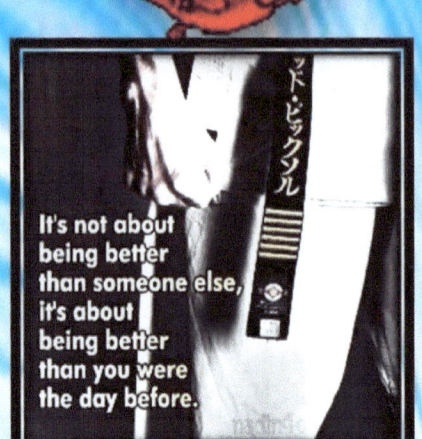

Classes:

Mon-Tue:	7:15 pm - 9:30 pm
Thu:	7:15 pm - 9:30 pm

JUST A REMINDER – Flying Dragons Taekwondo will be closed on Tuesdays until Tuesday August 7. We will still be open on Monday and Thursdays at the regular time!

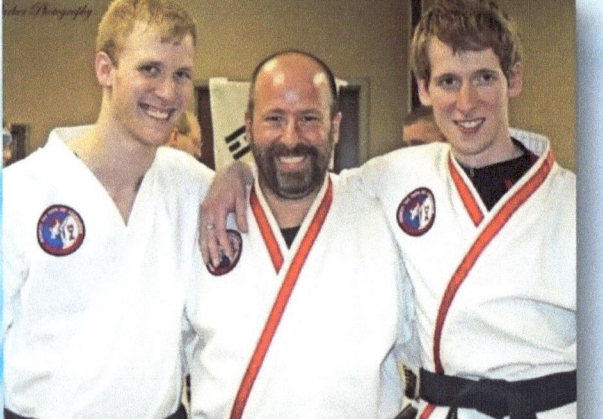

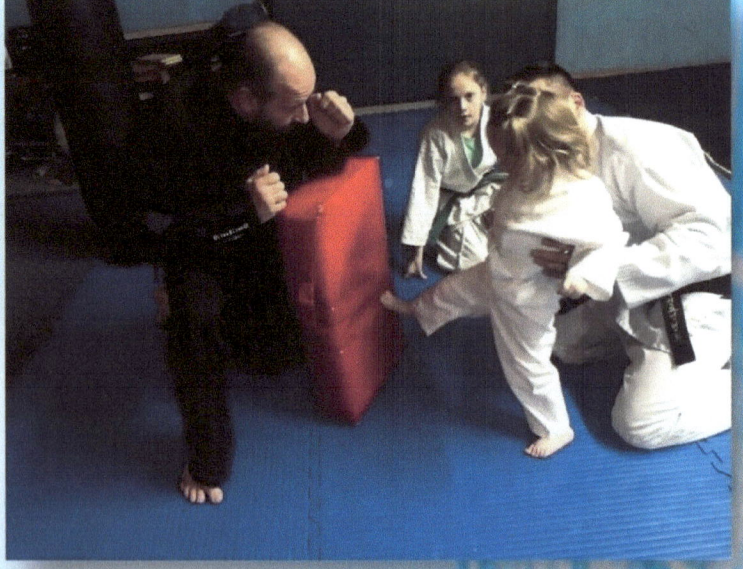

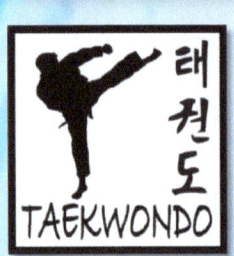

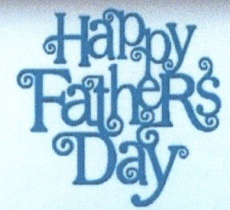

Founded in 1998 by Head Instructor Bart Nelson. The Flying Dragons Taekwondo and Mixed Martial Arts Training Center provides a home for those that wish to learn a way of life that

The Flying Dragons Taekwondo Training Center is run by Bart Nelson and his two sons: Dakota Nelson and Caleb Nelson